Vic Braden's
Quick Fixes

By Vic Braden and Robert Wool:

Vic Braden's Mental Tennis

Also by Vic Braden and Bill Bruns:

Vic Braden's Tennis for the Future

Teaching Children Tennis the Vic Braden Way

Vic Braden's Quick Fixes

Expert Cures for Common Tennis Problems

by Vic Braden and Bill Bruns

A *Sports Illustrated* Book

Little, Brown and Company
Boston, New York, Toronto, London

To Melody Braden

First Edition

Photographs by Melody Braden and Brent Root
Design by Margaret Saunders

Library of Congress Cataloging-in-Publication Data
Braden, Vic.
  Vic Braden's quick fixes : expert cures for common tennis problems / by Vic Braden and Bill Bruns.

  "A Sports illustrated book."
  ISBN 0-316-10514-7 (HC)
  ISBN 0-316-10515-5 (PB)
  I. Tennis — Miscellanea. I. Bruns, Bill. II. Title.
III. Title: Quick fixes.
GV995.B6859 1988
796.342'2 — dc19

10 9 8 7 6 5 4   KP

Sports Illustrated books
are published by
Little, Brown and Company
in association with
Sports Illustrated magazine

Published simultaneously in Canada
by Little, Brown & Company (Canada) Limited

Printed in the United States of America

ACKNOWLEDGMENTS

To Dr. Gideon Ariel, Dr. Sonny Cobble, Dr. Dave Costill, Dr. Jack Groppel, Greg Harney, Flo Hyman, Dr. Patrick Keating, Chris and Utami Kinard, Jack Kramer, Dr. James Loehr, Myron McNamara, Dr. Bruce Ogilvie, Dr. Ann Penny, Al Riedmayer, Steve Smith, Dr. Allen Stowe, Dr. Barry Unger, Julie Vollertson, the Aspen Ski Corporation, staff members of the Vic Braden Tennis College, and everyone who has shared coaching ideas with me over many years. We also want to thank our agent, John Boswell, whose own grievous problems playing tennis gave him a special interest in the fate of this project, and our editor, Bill Phillips, who never lost confidence in our original concept while providing vital editorial ideas.

CONTENTS

CHAPTER I

How to Make This Book Work for You

Ever since I began teaching tennis as a teenager on public courts in Kalamazoo, Michigan, thousands of players have asked me for tips to help their game. I've always had a keen interest in helping people improve, and being the flap-jaw that I am, I have usually had a lot of suggestions. Some of these people write me letters or call me on the phone or stop me in hotel lobbies, but most of them come through my tennis college, where they can sit in a classroom and ask quite serious questions about their backhand volleys or their forehand lobs.

I've now collected the most common and important questions and tried to answer them with the solutions that have worked best for me over the past forty years. These questions and solutions are organized by stroke (forehand, backhand, serve, service return, approach shot, volley, overhead, and lob), and a chapter is devoted to each stroke. So you should simply scan the table of contents, find your specific problem or problem area, and turn to my appraisal, where I provide the most likely reasons for that problem and some appropriate cures.

You may not find all your woes addressed here, but as you explore the material in each chapter you should start to recognize closely related problems that keep you from executing a particular stroke with power, accuracy, and consistency. I'm also assuming that you have been playing the game long enough to be able to identify the persistent problems that seem to keep you from beating better players. If you are just starting out (or if you need more in-depth and detailed coverage of particular strokes), please refer to my first book, *Tennis for the Future*, an instructional text that covers every aspect of the game in comprehensive detail.

To get the most effective use out of this book, try to view my problems-and-cures approach from several different perspectives.

I know, for example, that many of you will be looking for instant help—the secret little tips that can help make you famous by Friday. Indeed, the title of the book reflects the fact that I'm going straight to the heart of specific tennis ailments and offering first-aid type of advice. Many of these tips can certainly help improve your performance in a hurry by (1) correcting flaws in your swing that seem slight but are in fact significant and (2) providing key

checkpoints to keep in mind as you play, which can help solve particular problems that commonly arise.

In that sense, you should plan to use *Quick Fixes* as an easily accessible reference source that you can review before an important match or utilize as a courtside coaching companion when you practice or compete.

A second way to benefit from the advice in this book is to keep an open mind as you try to patch up a particular stroke with quick-fix cures. You may soon realize that the stroke needs a total revamping, in which case you can incorporate a number of tips relating to your specific problem area as you strive for permanent, long-term gains.

With these thoughts in mind, let's look at how you can best use my drills and techniques to actually improve your game—and enjoy the process.

1. Try to have a questioning, experimental approach to tennis.

The more you analyze my advice with a questioning mind—sitting back and asking yourself, "Does this make sense?"—the better you'll understand my approach to the game. Then all I ask is that you test out my various drills and suggestions and learn what actually happens when you swing the racket and move your body in unfamiliar, uncomfortable ways. As I tell all my students, "When you go to work on improving a stroke, you must try to feel good about feeling crummy, because the awkward feeling that accompanies new and accurate strokes is going to make you famous."

Also, when you're working on my suggested corrections out on the court in front of other people, don't be inhibited by how you think you look; if you're worrying about that, you won't feel free to experiment with the adjustments you need to incorporate into your swing.

2. Try to exaggerate any corrective techniques, whether they're in your swing or in your body movements.

I've noticed over the years that one reason so many people have trouble improving their stroking technique is that they only want to make tiny changes; if they normally bend their knees two inches on groundstrokes and I suggest they need to bend a lot more, they'll bend them three inches. If you settle for making minute changes like this, the law of regression will quickly take you back to your old way of hitting the ball, so you must exaggerate the desired new movements you find in this book in order to truly understand what the correct sensation feels like and how it affects the way you hit the ball. Then, if necessary, you can adjust.

3. Try different learning methods to gain a better sense of the stroking techniques stressed in this book.

We all learn a sport in slightly different ways, so experiment. If you're a kinesthetic learner, for example, try closing your eyes as you swing so you can focus on the desired sensations. Or, if you learn best through verbal advice, read my instructions aloud and ask yourself, "Do I really understand what he's saying?" I also find that many of my students benefit by swinging without a racket in their hands, since the racket often presents a foreign or distracting feeling as they try to learn a new movement. In a similar sense, if a particular segment of your swing is giving you trouble, just concentrate on what you should be doing in that segment, isolating it from the confusion of the overall swing.

4. Practice at home, especially if you don't have time to get out to practice between matches.

Throughout this book I'll be giving you various practice drills for checking your swing and improving your stroking technique. These are designed to help you detect and correct specific problems, and they can be done at home (in front of a mirror, for example) as easily as on the court. But as you try these corrective drills at home, be careful. I get letters from people who say, "I loved your tip but not the cost of a new lamp."

5. Try to sense the defenses that could be causing you to be resistant to change and keeping you from making important improvements.

If you're wondering how long it will take to correct specific problems in your stroking technique, here's a formula that applies to most people: the length of time it takes to make meaningful corrections is usually related to the strength of the defensive excuses you throw up as a screen. For example, some of my students, after about five minutes of hitting the ball into the net and over the back fence, will apologize by saying, "Normally I'm terrific, but my thyroid level is low this week." Then there are the players who hit the ball wild, grab their rackets, and mutter, "I don't know about graphite!" But the racket isn't the problem — it's the way the player is stroking the ball, and there's no way to hide from this reality.

6. Let your sense of humor come through as you work for improvements. "Laugh and win" is my motto.

Trying to master various aspects of the game can be fun and can bring you an unbelievable amount of satisfaction if you take the right attitude along the way. In my view, that means learning to laugh at your own klutziness and knowing that we all have the right to make mistakes as we try to improve. In the end, try to regard the tennis court as a "mistake center," not only when you play a match but also as you strive for better strokes. This approach will keep you on target for greater improvement and more victories.

7. In order to improve a stroke, you must be willing to break comfortable old habits that are holding you back, and this will require patience and persistence. So be fair to yourself.

Brain researchers tell us that it is relatively easy to program the mind to perform a new task but extremely difficult to deprogram it from something it has already learned. In tennis, that means that the longer you have played, the more your stroking patterns are set and the more difficult it may be to make the changes you seek. After all, the brain has programmed hundreds of different muscle groups in the process of "grooving" your strokes over the years, and now you're asking it to deprogram all those comfortable moves. That's not fair to the brain, which will resist your efforts to make a change and will continually try to revive your old bad habits. New strokes, therefore, take time to assimilate, for there's a tendency to get the new technique right for several swings and then lose it; but if you stick with the process, the swing will eventually fall into place.

Thus, when you start working on a particular stroke, with the help of my book, self-improvement should mean more to you than winning matches, for you must accept the fact that you will normally hit worse before you hit better. That's why it's so important to limit yourself to practice matches and hold off on the big-time events as you try to master any new, improved stroke. If you're playing a match and winning it is important to you, then it's only human nature that you should revert to your comfortable — and predictable — old stroking pattern, rather than fighting it out with a new swing that is causing you a lot of grief. The psychic pain of trying to do something new, under stress, that isn't proving successful, is simply too great in comparison to being comfortable with a stroking style you already know about — even though it, too, was unsuccessful.

Ultimately, if you want to break through to a higher playing level, concentrate on stroke production more than anything else. Many players, anxious to improve, try to cover all the bases and do everything they can think of; they plot intricate new strategies, eat granola, and study Zen — but they neglect to actually work on their tennis strokes. As a result, they continue to finish second in a field of two because they fail to get the racket head positioned correctly at impact, resulting in too many errors and weak shots. Stroke production should be your overriding concern, for the ball doesn't know that it's match point or that you're not wearing your lucky shorts — it only knows how the racket meets it at impact.

Very simply, if you can learn to hit a straight ball to your desired target area (ideally, your opponent's weak side or an open area on the court) with the desired length, either deep or short, that's all the strategy you'll ever need. The problem, of course, is that you can't always hit the ball where you want to hit it, especially with power. That's where this book will help improve and strengthen your game, so let's go to work and isolate your specific problems — and their appropriate cures. Then you can start packing your bags for Wimbledon.

CHAPTER 2

The Forehand

THE PROBLEM

"I'm hitting too many shots into the net."

REASONS:

A. Your racket face may be slightly closed (tilted down) at impact, rather than straight up and down. To check whether this is the case, freeze on a typical follow-through; then, without moving your wrist or elbow, lower your racket arm to the point where you contacted the ball. If the racket face is pointed down, it was closed when you hit, and whatever it takes to bring the racket back to a vertical position is the amount you moved it during the swing (most likely with a forearm roll).

B. Your racket may be too high as you start your forward swing into the ball. Always remember, the net is a high barrier—about 98 percent of us are too short to look over the net and see our opponent's baseline when we hit groundstrokes—and if you try to contact even a waist-level ball with a vertical racket face and an only slightly upward swing, the strong force of gravity can send your shot into the net.

C. Your upper body may be pulling around on a horizontal plane through impact [2-1 and 2-2]. Swinging like this creates a force that helps drive the ball lower than desired and turns you into a "net-cord hitter." Moreover, it contributes to a racket-roll problem, as seen in 2-2.

CURES:

A. Learn what it means to have a vertical racket face at impact. Stand in front of a fence or wall and take practice swings, stopping your racket at an imaginary impact point just short of the fence [2-3]. Make sure that the strings are vertical, with the racket edge straight up and down, then close your eyes and sense how it feels.

▶ Practice the drills and stroking patterns designed to help correct and prevent a destructive forearm roll in the hitting zone (especially those on page 19).

[2-1]   [2-2]

B. Get your racket head lower at the lowest point of the backswing to ensure a necessary low-to-high stroking motion into the ball. It's easy to think that we're getting low enough on the backswing, but it's difficult to overcome a natural tendency to keep the racket on the same level as the approaching ball (as we learn to do when hitting a baseball).

Here's a favorite drill to give you objective feedback and reinforce the low-to-high swing needed for topspin. Place a chair behind you and take your backswing [2-4], making sure that you graze the seat of the chair with the edge of your racket [2-5] before starting forward and up. Most chair seats are close to knee-height, and that's normally where you want the racket to go on the backswing. It's tough to swing down on a ball when the racket is this low at the beginning of your forward swing.

C. Work on the tips in this chapter that are designed to help you swing with a low-to-high motion and avoid pulling across the ball. A good starting point is to make sure that you are keeping your head down through impact, which helps stabilize your front side as you come through the ball. This also helps keep your hitting arm going out toward your intended target, not the side court.

THE PROBLEM

"Too many of my shots land too short."

I've long emphasized the importance of hitting the ball deep so you keep your opponent pinned behind the baseline, where he must beat you with good shots and fewer errors. If a strong opponent is driving you crazy by continually rushing the net and winning the point, it means that your groundstrokes are landing too short—closer to the service line than to the baseline. Even if your opponent ignores the opportunity to come to the net, these short groundstrokes are giving him easier balls to return.

REASONS:

A. Your racket may be too high at the lowest point of your backswing. Thus, instead of lifting the ball safely over the net with topspin, you are hitting with a relatively flat, horizontal swing. As a result, the harder you want to hit, the closer to the net you have to aim, and gravity is causing your shots to fall short.

B. You may have a natural forearm roll as you swing. This tends to smother the ball at impact, sending it short of your desired target area.

C. You may be pulling around with the front shoulder before impact. This creates a strong horizontal force that makes it almost impossible to contact the ball with the desired low-to-high motion, causing you instead to swing as though across a table-

top. Even if the ball goes over the net, it usually falls short because it has been hit on such a level plane.

D. As a topspin hitter, you may be swinging up at too steep an angle and imparting excessive topspin, which causes the ball to drop sharply and quickly as it clears the net.

CURES:

A. Make sure that you are elevating the ball properly by swinging on a low-to-high path and aiming for "air targets" at least four to six feet over the net. Notice that I must look *through* the net to see my opponent's court from the baseline [2-6]; the ball's perspective at impact is even lower [2-7]. If I try to hit straight across, how is this ball going to climb over the net? Thus, rather than consciously aiming for a target area on the court, I concentrate on hitting the ball through my appropriate "window" above the net [2-8]. Focusing on an elevated target like this will force you to swing on a low-to-high path, so you can hit the ball hard, with topspin, but still have it land deep and in play. At your next practice session, discover the window through which you must hit the ball to make it travel about 78 feet, from baseline to baseline. Simply have a friend stand at the net and hold up his racket as a visual reference point for your various forehand groundstrokes.

[2-6]

[2-7]

[2-8]

B. Counteract your forearm roll by consciously keeping the forearm fixed through impact and headed out toward your intended target area (as you can notice in 2-8). Remember my adage: "As the forearm goes, so goes the racket face."

C. To keep from pulling off the ball too early with your front shoulder, concentrate on staying "in" to the shot and swinging out and away from your body. This also facilitates hitting with a low-to-high motion. A good drill is to hold a ball out in front of your body at about head level and make your hitting hand go to the ball on the follow-through [2-9 and 2-10]. This will give you a perfect finish, with your upper arm and shoulder area touching your chin, and it will help you feel how the hitting hand should move as you swing into the ball.

D. If excessive topspin seems to be the cause of your problem, simply decrease the low-to-high angle of your forward stroke. Swing just as hard but hit through the ball on a lower forward path, more toward your opponent than toward the sky. As you do so, also make sure that you are elevating the ball high over the net so it can indeed travel deep. Ivan Lendl punishes the ball, yet many of his looping topspin drives still clear the net by eight or ten feet.

THE PROBLEM

"I keep hitting the ball beyond the baseline."

REASONS:

A. Almost always, this happens because the racket face is turned up (laid back slightly) at impact.

B. You may be hitting too hard, with insufficient topspin rotation to bring the ball down in time.

CURES:

A. In order to have a vertical racket face at impact, make sure that your racket is slightly hooded (turned down) at the lowest point of your backswing. When the racket is positioned like this [2-11], you may think, "This dumb shot is going to hit me in the foot!" But having the hitting palm facing down as you take the arm back guarantees that the racket face

will be perfect at impact [2-12], provided that you don't get "wristy" as you come into the ball. To groove this critical technique into your forehand stroke, hold the racket face against a fence or wall at your normal contact point. Now take the racket backward — without any wrist adjustment — and notice that the face should be pointed downward at the lowest point of the backswing. Then swing toward the fence, stopping at your contact point and checking that the racket is absolutely vertical and not turned up. Keep swinging like this to get a good feel for what should be happening.

▶ If your racket face is turned up at impact, you may also be leaning back as you contact the ball [2-13], so make sure that you are leaning in, with your front shoulder out over the front foot [2-14].

[2-11]

[2-12]

Step out to meet the ball instead of letting the ball come to you.

B. Increase the upward angle of your low-to-high stroke to impart greater topspin rotation and produce a shorter shot with the same power input.

One of the many virtues of topspin is that if you start hitting topspin groundstrokes beyond the baseline you don't have to ease up to get the ball in play. Instead, just keep lifting more toward the sky until you find the low-to-high angle that works for you. If you are swinging at an upward angle of about 30 degrees and are knocking the ball out, then increase the spin by swinging at a 45-degree angle. Your shots should now start landing safely in play, even though you are hitting with the same racket speed.

[2-13]

[2-14]

THE PROBLEM

"I can't seem to hit the ball with topspin."

REASONS:

A. You may be trying to roll your racket head up and over the ball to impart topspin. That's the advice many famous playing pros have given people over the years, because that's how they *think* they generate topspin. But it's a misleading feel, and this effort to use considerable wrist and forearm action and racket manipulation to hit topspin can create a destructive stroking motion, especially at the club level.

B. On the backswing, you may not be getting the racket head lower than the intended point of impact in order to hit up the back side of the ball.

C. You may be swinging at a desired low-to-high angle into the ball, but at still too flat a trajectory. Our studies show that hitting the ball on a 17-degree upward-swing path is sufficient only to remove the topspin that has been imparted to the incoming shot by the bounce. (Every ball gains this forward rotation as it comes off the court.)

CURES:

A. Remember: topspin can be hit only one way, with a racket face that is vertical at impact and moving on a low-to-high path. A rolling forearm motion in the hitting zone is meaningless, since the ball is on the strings for only about four milliseconds — not enough time for "wrist-rolling" action to have any effect on the ball's spin. Certain pros appear to be using a lot of wristy action to impart heavy topspin, but when we study them through high-speed photography — frame by frame — we find that the wrist and the forearm are a fixed unit at impact and that the racket head is vertical but moving forward and up at the ball.

B. The racket face must be well below the intended point of contact as you begin swinging forward and up toward the incoming ball, as indicated by the X's on the fence in the picture sequence [2-15 through 2-17]. This stroking pattern imparts topspin rotation.

[2-15]

[2-16]

[2-17]

C. In order to generate sufficient topspin on hard-hit forehands, you must swing toward the sky at an upward angle of at least 30 degrees. Ideally, however, you should strive to swing at a 45-degree angle or more in order to hit hard, deep, accurate shots from baseline to baseline. You may be thinking, "If I actually swing up like that, my shots are going to land on the moon." But as you practice, see for yourself that the ball actually does come down into play, assuming you have a vertical racket face at impact.

THE PROBLEM

"I have a giant racket, but I still hit a lot of shots off the edge of the frame."

Do you have trouble consistently hitting the "sweet spot" on your strings—even with an over-sized racket? And does this make you think, "Yeah, I must have terrible eyes; I can't seem to stay focused on the ball"?

REASON:

Actually, your head may be the culprit here, not your eyes. We've found in our high-speed photography research that if you look up just before impact, the racket also moves, causing you to hit the ball near the edge of the frame.

CURES:

▶ Be patient as you complete the stroke. Instead of worrying about what your opponent is doing on the other side of the net, concentrate on following the ball into the hitting zone and leaving your head down until your hitting shoulder or upper arm touches your chin [2-18]. The follow-through happens so fast that you'll have plenty of time to see where your shot is traveling, well before it reaches the net.

▶ Find a cue that will help keep you from abruptly pulling up off the shot just before impact. This should guarantee more "on-center" hits. For example:

▶ Don't raise your head to track your shot until you hear the ball meet the racket.

▶ Since nobody is capable of seeing the ball actually hit the strings, concentrate on watching the racket or your arm cross in front of your body before you look up.

▶ Some players find it useful to visualize an X on the court, below the point of impact, as I'm doing in the photograph.

▶ Count "one thousand one" *after* you hit the ball (at first you may find that you have a tendency to start counting even before impact).

▶ If you keep your belly-button facing toward the side fence as you hit, instead of pulling around early, you'll have a hard time moving your head too soon.

[2-18]

▶ Since our research shows that many players literally close their eyes before impacting the ball (usually a signal to the brain that the shot is over), consciously try to keep your eyes open as you make contact. Strive to get a picture of how the ball is coming in and where you're contacting it, and I'll bet you'll start hitting better, more consistent shots.

THE PROBLEM

"When I try to go down the line against a cross-court shot, the ball tends to go wide into the doubles alley."

REASONS:

A. If you're taking an opponent's cross-court shot and trying to go "down the line" (straight), the ball may be coming off the racket at a deflected angle toward the doubles alley. Unless you compensate, the ball always leaves the racket at the same angle at which it arrives—in accordance with the physical principle of incident reflected angles.

B. Your hitting arm may be coming through late, and the racket face actually pointing out of bounds at impact. The most likely culprit: a wrist "layback" problem [2-19], caused by taking too rapid a backswing and playing with a loose wrist.

[2-20]

[2-19]

CURES:

A. When returning an opponent's cross-court shot, you must counteract the ball's deflection off your racket when you try to hit a down-the-line return. For example, if you tend to swing softly and the ball is arriving at a good pace, aim about halfway between the point where your opponent contacted the ball and your intended target area (just about at my opponent's feet in 2-20). But if you hit hard, aim closer to your down-the-line target area (near the X on the net in 2-20). This should compensate for the deflected angle and allow your shot to land in the desired baseline corner.

[2-21]

B. Correct your wrist layback problem by leading with a raised hitting elbow on your backswing [2-21]. This will allow the racket to stay in sync with your rotating body and meet the ball at the appropriate spot.

THE PROBLEM

"I have no control; the ball goes everywhere—into the net, long, short, and wide."

REASONS:

A. You may be using a Continental grip, which often contributes to erratic and unpredictable shot-making from the baseline (especially in club tennis).

B. Your forearm may be rolling over as it comes through the hitting zone.

Both of these factors lead to excessive racket-head "play" that is difficult to control; when your timing is a fraction off, your game can easily unravel.

If you're presently using a Continental grip, notice that the palm is positioned more on top of the racket handle [2-22] than it is in the desired Eastern [2-23] or semi-Western grip [2-24]. This positioning of the hand often causes the racket face to be pointed toward the sky on the backswing. People say, "That's no problem—I'll just roll the racket and have it correct at impact." But this requires exquisite timing, since the ball "sits" on the strings for just an instant. In fact, when you roll your racket in the hitting zone, there is only about 15-milliseconds' leeway to execute a reasonably good shot. Beating this margin of error—consistently—requires that you have much greater natural talent in order to play the game well than if you always have the racket face fixed at impact by using an Eastern or semi-Western grip.

CURES:

A. If you presently hold a Continental, you can greatly reduce the adjustments it imposes on your stroke by switching to the Eastern or semi-Western grip.

As you learn to hold a new grip, take time to concentrate on letting go of the grip and then re-gripping (in your living room and as you practice your groundstrokes) so you acquire a feel for the correct grip when you switch between your forehand and backhand.

B. Maintain a firm wrist and forearm from the beginning of your backswing through impact. Check to make sure that the racket face and the hitting palm are pointed *downward* at the lowest point of your backswing [2-25]; this frees you to swing up through the shot with a fixed wrist and forearm, knowing that the racket face will be vertical at impact [2-26] without any adjustments necessary in the hitting zone.

▶ Once you have established a desired grip, make sure that the forearm is going out in line with your intended target area as you swing into the ball, thus helping prevent a forearm roll, which in turn produces a racket roll.

[2-22]

[2-23]

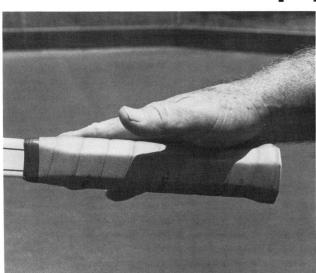

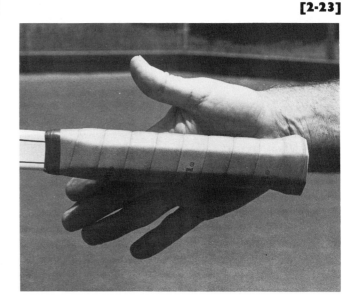

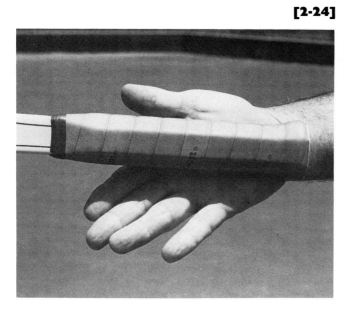

THE PROBLEM

"Dinkers drive me crazy."

Are you an unpredictable type of player who has a good day on the court Wednesday, a terrible day Saturday, but a great day Sunday? If so, then you very likely prefer opponents who hit the ball hard but with an even pace. Conversely, your game probably comes unraveled against a "dinker," who hits the ball slow and slower, with a variety of elevations and spins.

REASON:

You're a wrist-roller, pal, and it means that you're horsing around with the racket head in the hitting zone [2-27] instead of having it in a fixed position. Thus you tend to fare best against hard hitters who have a consistent rhythm and predictability to their groundstrokes, which helps you sense just when to roll your forearm into the shot. The dinker, however, drives you nuts because his shots bounce differently every time; one time you roll the racket too early, the next time too late. The reason, very simply, is that in 15 milliseconds—all the time you have in which to actually contact the ball and be accurate— you can't roll the forearm and accurately time the impact, one shot after another.

[2-27]

[2-28]

CURES:

▶ Reevaluate your grip and settle on one that helps ensure a vertical racket head at impact, one hit after another, against any type of opponent. Your investigation should eliminate the Continental and lead you to the Eastern or semi-Western grip.

▶ Check that your racket face is angled down on the backswing so you don't need to make any adjustments to have a vertical racket at impact. Notice, for example, that when the racket is straight up and down on the backswing [2-28], the racket face is turned up at impact [2-29]—unless you adjust by rolling the forearm.

[2-29]

▶ Since the forearm is the key to racket-head control, keep it going out toward your intended target area through impact. This ensures that the wrist is fixed and the racket face isn't rolling over in the hitting zone.

Learn to swing only from the shoulder joint to minimize racket-head play and keep from rolling your forearm into the shot. As a drill [2-30 through 2-32], hold a weight in your hitting hand and swing freely from the shoulder—like a bowler, making sure the arm finishes "up and out," away from your body. The extra weight (a racket weighs less than one pound) will help you sense what it means to avoid a forearm roll.

THE PROBLEM

"I usually pull the ball cross-court when I want to hit it straight."

I talked in chapter 1 about the fact that to play tennis well you must learn to hit a straight ball to your opponent's weak side or to an open area on the court—and hit it with the desired length, either deep or short. This is elementary, I know, but most people have trouble hitting the ball straight when they want it to go straight. They know there's an opening, but they can't hit the ball to this opening. Instead they hit the ball close to their opponent or out of bounds.

REASONS:

A. Your racket may be rolling over in the hitting zone, causing you to pull across—toward the cross-court [2-33] instead of toward your intended target area. You may in fact be swinging as if you intend to play an opponent standing in an adjoining court.

B. You may be pulling around with the front shoulder before impact, creating a horizontal "hula hoop" motion (as I showed in 2-1 and 2-2). This generates a horizontal force away from your target and makes it virtually impossible to compensate by adjusting the racket face in the hitting zone. Your swing fails to reflect the fact that a tennis court must be viewed as a long, narrow sidewalk, not a wide expanse.

C. Your elbow may be too close to your body as you go to contact the ball [2-34]. When the arm is scrunched in like this, you're forced to swing with a rolling forearm motion instead of letting the arm travel freely out toward your target.

D. Feeling a pinch, the upper segment of your hitting arm may be stopping just before impact. This causes the forearm segment to roll over, bringing the racket face across on a horizontal plane.

[2-33]

[2-34]

CURES:

A. Swing out away from your body, on a low-to-high path, so your racket can stay in line with your intended target. Notice in the photographs [2-35 through 2-37] that I'm using a line on the court to check my swing. Stand with both feet on a line like this and practice keeping the racket traveling on the same side of that line, from the backswing through the follow-through. Visualize that same relationship with the line as you actually play. You should also take practice swings with your back against the fence. If you can avoid hitting the barrier with your racket on the backswing (unless you're intentionally using extra body rotation) and on the follow-through, you have a good, controlled swing that keeps all of your important movements going toward the intended target area. *(continued)*

[2-35]

▶ The palm is your guidance control on the forehand, so make sure that it's setting the proper course by traveling out toward the net post at impact [2-38]. Check your follow-through: if your palm is still out in line with your target area, it means that you were "tracking" properly through impact and insuring yourself against pulled shots. (The racket itself should be angled to the outside of your target.)

B. Think about my "third eye" concept as a way to help keep your front shoulder and front hip from pulling around. Pretend that your belly button is your third eye and that it must see the ball at impact [2-39]—not your opponent.

▶ Check that your non-hitting hand is either out in front of your body or actually coming in toward your body as you contact the ball. If, instead, the hand is pulling around away from your body, then it's contributing to an unwanted horizontal force as you rotate into the shot.

C. Strive to contact the ball off your front foot so your hitting elbow can be comfortably away from

[2-39]

your body as you come through the shot (as I'm demonstrating in 2-38).

D. Instead of unconsciously allowing the upper segment of your hitting arm to stop just before impact, focus on having the arm come through on a radius as you swing, using the upper shoulder like a hinge.

▶ Try to gain that crucial feeling of letting the racket fall low on the backswing—with the palm turned down and the wrist firmly cocked [2-40]— and then swinging up through the ball and out and away from your body. Just let your arm swing easily from the shoulder so it flows freely toward your intended target area rather than pulling across your body. A good way to focus on what it means to swing with a loose shoulder segment—with the shoulder joint as the central point of the radius—is to stand with your non-hitting hand behind your back as you take a swing. When you can go out to meet the ball and keep the upper arm from slowing down, everything tends to fall nicely into place.

THE PROBLEM

"I often feel cramped as I hit the ball."

When I watch club players in baseline rallies, I'm struck by how often they are "crowded" by the ball as they go to swing, even when they have enough time to reach and prepare for shots that come to them along the baseline. As a result, they're inhibited in or prevented from swinging aggressively and effectively at the ball.

REASONS:

If you often don't feel in control as you hit your forehand, check for these bad habits:

A. You may be allowing the ball to come to you, instead of making sure that you go out to meet it early.

B. You may not be arriving at your hitting position early enough to effect a smooth, unhurried forward stroke. Perhaps your sense of timing is off; instead of trying to reach your hitting position as early as possible, you may subconsciously be trying to arrive there at the same time as the ball. You may also be letting your feet "fall asleep."

C. You may be waiting too long to start your backswing. You may be arriving at the ball in time but timing the start of your backswing to the bounce rather than according to the shot's incoming trajectory.

D. Your swing may be too long, perhaps as a result of wrist layback [2-41].

CURES:

A. Start thinking about going out to "greet" the ball, as though to shake hands with a friend. This image should help you move much earlier to get into position so you can step forward into the ball as you swing.

My coin drill can help you learn to position your feet so you're ready to put your full weight into the shot and make contact before the ball gets too close to your body. Simply drop a coin on the court (indicated by the X in 2-42) and practice moving into position to hit, landing next to the coin with your back foot and stepping forward with the front foot

[2-41]

[2-42]

24

toward the shot. This forces you to learn a little skipping motion that gets your feet properly positioned and makes you think about going out to meet the ball.

B. Try to take a quick first step toward the ball as soon as you see it leave your opponent's racket. If you arrive at the ball a little early, no problem—just delay your forward motion into the ball. A perfect drill is to have your practice partner stand at the baseline and hit groundstrokes while you try to make a decision and start moving by the time the ball reaches his service line.

C. Unless you're still running to the ball, start your backswing before your opponent's shot reaches the net, especially on a fast surface and against a hard hitter. When practicing this early backswing, try to exaggerate by starting your swing sooner than would seem appropriate; you'll very likely be perfect.

▶ Make sure that you are initiating the backswing by rotating your upper body away from the net [2-43], as opposed to just taking the racket back.

[2-43]

Shoulder rotation helps guarantee early preparation by automatically bringing back the racket.

D. On the backswing, the racket should travel no farther back than pointing just about straight at the back fence, unless you are deliberately using extra trunk rotation. To check it, try this: when your racket is back and you're ready to uncoil into the shot [2-44], can you see the racket face with peripheral vision—without turning your head? If you can, then your backswing is probably right on the money.

If wrist layback is causing you to take an excessively long backswing, the best correction is to push or raise your elbow up and away from your body on the backswing [2-44]. This will automatically shorten your swing and provide greater racket control as you go to hit the ball. You may even want to wait for your groundstrokes with the bend already in your elbow. Then all you have to do is turn and hit, remembering to rotate your upper body. You'll see most top players lead with the elbow going back because it shortens the swing and prevents wrist layback. It may look funny, but it's one reason those players are on the tour and you're in the stands.

THE PROBLEM

"I keep the ball in play, but I can't seem to hit with much power."

REASONS:

A. You may be letting the ball get too close to your body, which cramps your swing [2-45] and reduces the length of your stroking radius—thus reducing your potential power.

B. You may be hitting with an isolated arm movement, perhaps not realizing that most power in tennis is derived from the trunk of the body.

C. You may think you have a nice, fluid forehand stroke, but if your opponents are not afraid of your forehand, then wrist layback may be undermining your efforts by putting your racket out of synchronization with your rotating body.

D. You may be hitting with a straight-back swing, as opposed to the desired loop, which means that you lose the benefits of gravity acting on a falling racket head (i.e., the further it falls, the faster it is moving as you start forward) and you have only a comparatively short distance in which to generate racket-head speed coming into impact.

E. You may not be blocking the body's front-side rotation as your hitting arm approaches the hitting zone, which allows the racket to gain significant velocity. As a result, you're losing the body's natural whipping action, which can make the racket snap hard through impact.

CURES:

A. Whenever possible, reach a hitting position early enough to step into the ball and contact it comfortably away from your body and off the front foot [2-46]. Ideally, the distance between your body and hitting elbow should be roughly equal to the distance between your outspread pinkie and thumb, so you can be in control while maximizing the radius of your stroke. This also allows you to shift your weight forward into the shot, transferring this power out and away from your body—toward your intended target—as you uncoil into the shot.

B. Rather than "arming" the ball over the net, get your body involved in the stroke so you can capitalize on the natural whipping action it generates in the hitting arm. Very simply, hitting power derives from

racket-head speed at impact, and that speed is largely created by the correct utilization of the body segments —not by a muscular arm.

More specifically, once you have initiated the backswing by rotating your upper body, let the body's natural uncoiling action make you famous. This is the kinetic chain, where the key body segments —knees, hips, trunk, shoulders, and hitting arm— turn and uncoil into the shot in that sequence, just slightly ahead of the racket. However, this action becomes a significant source of energy only if the body's segments uncoil—and stop—in the proper sequence. The principle of deceleration-acceleration is at work here: when one segment stops, the next segment speeds up.

C. Avoid the destructive effects of wrist layback by starting your backswing early, with upper-body rotation (as opposed to simply taking the arm back on its own), and by keeping your elbow up and away from your body as you go back. This will shorten your swing and keep the racket face moving in sync with

[2-45]

your rotating body as you come into the ball, allowing these forces to flow together out toward your intended target area.

D. Since a stroke's power is related to how fast the racket is moving at impact, learn to hit with a loop backswing instead of taking the racket straight back down to its lowest point before moving forward into the ball. Thanks to physics, this looping action—taking the racket back at about eye level [2-47] and letting it fall—generates about 11 miles per hour in racket speed at the lowest point of the loop. The person who goes straight back has "gained" zero miles per hour at that point and cannot generate maximum racket-head speed until several feet *after* hitting the ball.

E. Let the stopping power of your front shoulder make your hitting arm famous. As you uncoil into the ball, abruptly stop your front shoulder when the racket is about two feet from impact. This allows the hitting arm to come whipping through and make the racket snap.

[2-46]

One good way to stop this upper-body rotation at the right moment is to use the non-hitting hand as a brake by bringing it in toward your body just before impact. Or you may want to emulate Chris Evert, whose left hand is out in front of her body just before she hits. This helps keep her left side from pulling around on a horizontal rotation and transferring energy away from her intended target area. It's also useful to think about stopping your belly button just before contact (the "third eye" concept; see page 22). This sudden stop gives you a boost by turning the arm and the racket into a whip.

THE PROBLEM

"I just don't have my touch today."

When you try to win with "touch" — those unique last-second adjustments in your swing or with the wrist as you try to control or "guide" the shot — your forehand is vulnerable on any given day, at any given point in the match. The problem is the margin for error this leaves in the hitting zone. To hit wristy forehands successfully, you need incredible timing because the racket head must be vertical at impact on one hit after another. Change the angle of the racket face at impact by as little as two or three degrees, and the point is often over and your opponent is smiling.

REASONS:

How well you contact the ball in the hitting zone is only as good as the preparation and the approach you had to the ball. It's not your touch at impact that controls the ball, but what takes place *before* impact — your ability to have the racket moving and facing in the right direction as you reach the hitting zone. So if your forehand is unreliable and unpredictable, chances are excellent that:

A. You may be adding too much racket-head play to your stroke.

B. You may be trying to manipulate the ball at impact, when it's already too late to make conscious adjustments.

CURES:

A. Keep your swing compact — short and simple, stripped of unnecessary little flourishes — so your hitting shoulder, forearm, and wrist can move in unison and work as one unit.

One good drill for this is to hold your non-hitting arm behind your body [2-48] as you practice swinging freely from the shoulder joint, out toward your target area, while maintaining a fixed racket head and a firm wrist. Close your eyes and concentrate on what it means to have only the shoulder joint working, like a well-oiled hinge.

▶ Make sure that the racket face is hooded at the lowest point of your backswing so you're free to go forward and up with a fixed wrist and forearm.

[2-48]

▶ Hold an Eastern or semi-Western grip, rather than a Continental. I offered my rationale for this in the tip on pages 16–17.

B. Instead of thinking that you can get away with fancy wrist movements just before impact, concentrate on keeping the racket head stable as you "play" with your body. Many players get into trouble by doing just the opposite: freezing the important body movements (e.g., of the thighs, hips, and trunk) and playing with the racket face. Relying on the wrist simply leaves you too vulnerable to the unpredictable moments of a typical tennis match.

CHAPTER 3

The Backhand

THE PROBLEM

"I scatter my backhand shots."

[3-3]
[3-4]

REASON:

If your backhand is rarely predictable, landing too short one time and too long the next, then you have excessive racket-head play in the hitting zone. Remember, a one-degree racket turn can make a difference of five or six feet in where the ball lands on some shots, just as it can on the forehand.

CURES:

▶ Hold an Eastern backhand grip [3-1 and 3-2] by moving your hitting palm to the top of the racket

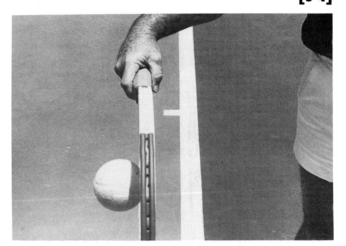

[3-1] [3-2]

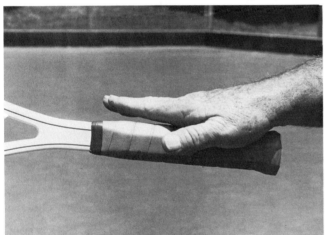

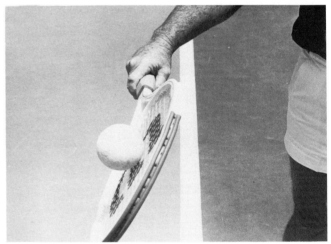

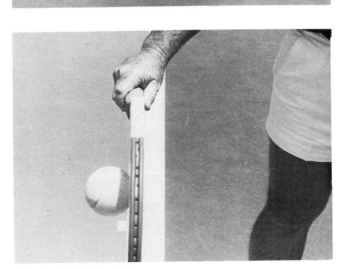

grip. This provides more stability at impact than any other grip and requires less wrist adjustment in order to produce a vertical racket head at contact, thus helping to minimize errors. Notice, for instance, that I must adjust my wrist when I hold a Continental in order to have the racket face vertical at impact [3-3]. Without this awkward adjustment, the racket face is open at impact [3-4] and requires a wrist-rolling effort in the hitting zone—unless you are trying to hit with underspin. This helps explain why many players opt for a defensive, underspin backhand.

▶ Strengthen your extensor muscles (which lie atop the arm when your palm is facing down) to increase racket-head control at impact. This strength is

especially important as the match progresses and your hitting arm begins to tire. A good daily drill is to take backhand practice swings with a cover on the racket to provide resistance. After every three or four swings, rest your arm briefly and give it a good shake to prevent muscle strain. Gradually increase the weight resistance by putting a tennis ball inside the racket cover and adding another one every several weeks [3-5]. Another easy but effective exercise is to squeeze an old tennis ball with your hand laid back and the arm extended so you can see and feel the extensor muscles working. (Punch a hole in the ball so it provides a greater range of motion as you squeeze.)

▶ Concentrate on keeping the racket head fixed and the wrist locked tight as you rotate your body into the shot. This will help you avoid a downfall of the many club players who tend to swing with a rigid body while letting the wrist go loose.

▶ Try playing with two hands on the racket. The second hand helps brace the racket for greater control and helps guarantee a vertical racket face at impact. (See the tip on pages 50–51.)

THE PROBLEM

"I hit into the net too often."

REASONS:

When the net keeps stopping your backhand drives (as opposed to when you try to hit with underspin), consider these three basic flaws:

A. Your racket face may be turned slightly down as you contact the ball.

B. Your racket may be too high at the lowest point of your backswing. Although the racket face may be vertical at impact, you're swinging too "flat" (i.e., relatively straight across through the ball), and gravity is pulling the ball down.

C. You may be trying to hit "net-skimmers," rather than lifting the ball over that high net with topspin (again, assuming you are driving the ball hard).

CURES:

A. Keep your hitting arm fixed and extended through impact, with the racket face straight up and down at contact.

   To learn whether you are rolling the racket over in the hitting zone, freeze on the follow-through, then lower your hitting arm back to the approximate contact point, allowing movement only at the shoulder joint. If the racket face isn't vertical (and if you're holding an Eastern backhand grip, as I recommend), then you haven't maintained a firm wrist position; whatever it takes to set the racket face properly vertical is the amount you have rolled it during the swing. Another good check is to swing against a fence and stop at your normal impact point to see whether the racket face is vertical [3-6]. Using a fence provides important feedback on the backhand: you can't accurately see the racket's vertical position when it's out in front of the body at impact.

B. Check that your racket is dropping lower on the backswing than the intended point of contact, so you can have a natural low-to-high lifting motion. Since we all have trouble visualizing what the racket is doing on the backswing as it goes out of sight, have a friend watch as you take a practice swing. Tell him when you think your racket has reached its lowest point, for you may find that when you say "Now!"—thinking the racket is down around your kneecaps—it's actually higher than your waist. If so, try to

[3-6]

exaggerate getting your racket arm low (facilitated by good knee bend) as you work to swing into the ball with a low-to-high motion.

   A favorite drill here [3-7 through 3-9] is to visualize an X on your back thigh as you take your backswing. Have the non-hitting hand ride lightly on the racket throat going back, and practice letting both arms drop toward that imaginary X—always touching the back thigh with the second hand before you start your forward and upward swing. You may be surprised at how few times you actually touch the thigh unless you make a determined effort to do so (of course, this should be a smooth and continuous motion when you are actually swinging at a ball). Also try my sit-and-hit chair drill (pages 46–47), where you place a chair behind you and make sure your racket edge grazes the seat on the backswing before you start forward and up.

C. In baseline rallies, aim for a target window above the net [3-10] rather than a target area on the court, which you can see only through the net. This will

[3-10]

shift your visual attention away from the net tape—which is catching so many of your shots—and encourage you to hit with a much greater safety margin. Here again, just as on the forehand, the eyes affect the muscle system; there's a tendency to hit where your eyes are looking. In studies using the Eye Mark Recorder, a device that films where players' pupils are directed during play, we found that the net tape is one of the most distracting elements on court. Often players were looking right at the tape as they aimed their shots. So now, as you work to elevate your backhand drives, remember my face in the window frame about six feet above the net.

The desire to hit "net-skimmers" is a common one in club tennis, where players often talk about wanting to imitate Jimmy Connors's hard, low backhand. While Jimmy indeed swings at less of an upward, forward angle than most other pros, he complains that he can't get the depth that he seeks when he plays the ball too close to the net. As hard as he hits, his groundstrokes land around the service line unless he elevates the ball properly.

THE PROBLEM

"I keep hitting the ball too short."

If this is your problem, you're losing out on two fronts. Ideally you should be pounding the ball deep enough to keep a smart opponent pinned behind the baseline, where he can't really hurt you, while you wait for the first opportunity to attack his weak groundstrokes. Conversely, if you find that an aggressive opponent is continually coming to the net and putting YOU on the defensive, then you're giving him too many approach-shot opportunities with weak backhands that tend to land around the service line.

REASONS:

A. Your racket may still be too high at the lowest point of your backswing. This means that you are contacting the ball with too level a swing, which forces you to aim the ball close to the net in order to keep it in play when you try to hit hard. The force of gravity is so strong that it's going to pull the ball down earlier than you want, either short or into the net.

B. You may be relying too much on the hitting arm for power, which usually makes the ball go short.

C. You may be rolling the forearm over in the hitting zone, which tends to smother the shot.

D. If you're a topspin hitter, you may be swinging up at too steep an angle. This means that the ball is not being depressed sufficiently at impact and thus travels with an increased number of revolutions, resulting in a sharper and shorter arc over the net.

▶ In a similar vein, you may also be hitting either too much off the back foot or while pushing back off the front foot. This tends to cause players to lift up into the shot at a steeper angle and to bring the racket up too quickly, which almost always produces a short ball.

CURES:

A. As I'm demonstrating in the photographs, make sure that you are getting your racket low enough on

[3-11]

[3-12]

the backswing [3-11] to be able to hit with a low-to-high lifting motion [3-12], which allows you to drive the ball hard and deep but safely over the net.

B. Learn to utilize — and emphasize — the power of an uncoiling body (as detailed starting on page 52), even with a short, controlled backswing.

C. Maintain a firm, extended hitting arm through impact so you can hit the ball properly, with a racket face that is consistently and correctly positioned.

D. Decrease the low-to-high angle at which you swing into the ball to drive your shots safely deeper.

▶ Contact the ball with your weight transferring out onto your front foot [3-13] so you maximize your chances of hitting the ball hard and deep with topspin. Then simply adjust your upward hitting angle to keep reproducing these desired deep shots. A forward follow-through like this also leaves you in position to move in quickly if you see that your backhand is going to give your opponent trouble.

[3-13]

THE PROBLEM

"I seem to sky the ball a lot."

REASONS:

When your backhands are high, ineffective shots that often go out of play, the culprit is not the low-to-high swing that I advocate. Instead, other flaws in your hitting technique are creating the root problem —a racket face that is turned up or slightly opened at impact, rather than straight up and down. These flaws include:

▶ Your grip may be too far toward the forehand side. If you're holding a Continental grip, the racket face has a much greater tendency to turn up and sky the ball—unless you make a difficult adjustment. To keep from hitting high balls with a Continental, you must compensate either by pushing the wrist forward

more or by raising the hitting elbow. Otherwise, even with a perfect stroke, the bottom edge of the racket will be turned up at impact.

▶ Even with an Eastern backhand grip, your racket face may be pointing skyward at impact because your hitting shoulder is leaning back as you come into the ball, which tilts the racket face up [3-14].

▶ Your hitting *elbow* may be raised and leading the way as you approach the ball [3-15].

▶ You may be standing stiff-kneed as you swing, and simply dropping the racket head low by loosening your wrist. As a result, you must "bevel" the racket face (lay it back slightly) in order to lift the ball up and over the net.

[3-14]

[3-15]

CURES:

▶ Hold an Eastern backhand grip. If you're currently playing with a Continental, move your palm toward the top of the racket grip (as shown in 3-1). This will help keep you from "skying" so many shots.

▶ Step into the ball and make sure that the hitting shoulder is leading the way and leaning forward— not falling back—as you contact the ball (as shown in 3-13). Also notice that my hitting arm is extended as I lean into the shot and that my front shoulder is leading the way, not the hitting elbow.

▶ Strive to finish with your weight transferred to the front foot and your hitting shoulder out over the foot on the follow-through [3-16]. A good reminder is to visualize a plumb line dropping from your hitting shoulder and finishing ahead of your front foot.

▶ Check to be sure that you're bending your knees enough to allow for a desired low-to-high stroke. Good knee bend allows you to hit with a natural lifting motion and the absence of any adaptive movements with the racket face as you come through on the swing.

THE PROBLEM

"My shots often travel off target to the left."

REASONS:

A. Most likely you have an unnecessarily long backswing [3-17], which causes the racket head to come around late into the shot and trail the body at impact, sending the ball off target to the left. This is a typical problem for the many club players who think they should take the racket way back in order to hit with power but fail to coil their body as they do so.

B. Like many club players, you could be delaying your backswing too long, thus setting up a late swing into the ball. As a result, you may be leading with your hitting elbow as you come into the ball [3-18]. This type of elbow action raises the racket and lays the face back, causing misdirected hits. A "slapping elbow" not only undermines a good backhand but can eventually lead to tendinitis, also known as "tennis elbow."

[3-17]

[3-18]

[3-19]

[3-20]

CURES:

A. Keep the racket—and your arms—traveling (1) on a vertical plane into the shot while (2) staying on the front (belly-button) side of your body. This means letting shoulder rotation, or body coil, take the racket back. Think about turning your upper body to initiate the backswing, rather than simply taking the racket back on its own. Notice that I lead with the non-hitting elbow as I take the racket back [3-19]; this helps control the backswing and keeps the racket from going too far behind the body.

If you have a wraparound backswing, you may be misinterpreting what you think the pros are doing. Certain top players have their racket pulled well behind their body on the backswing, but have you noticed the body coil that accompanies this? Shoulder and trunk rotation (as opposed to a longer arm swing) is what counts, for it automatically brings the racket back farther, but only as part of a relatively short, controlled swing [3-20].

As a drill, practice keeping your backswing and

(continued)

[3-21]

your forward movement into the ball on a vertical, low-to-high path by working with your back to a fence [3-21 through 3-23]. The fence will give you instant feedback as you try to keep from hitting it with your backswing (unless you have good body coil, which takes the racket back farther but does it in sync with your body) and your follow-through. In addition, it will keep you from coming around on a horizontal plane.

B. Don't get lazy with your body. Since backhand drives—notably those hit with topspin—should be contacted much farther out ahead of the body (toward the net) than forehands, make sure that you are starting your backswing early enough. You want to have time to go out to meet the ball and make contact comfortably out in front of your body with an extended hitting arm [3-24] while pivoting properly with your body. Extending your hitting arm like a stick on the backswing and leaving it in that position, using only the shoulder joint as you swing [3-25], may feel funny, but it looks great—and it's effective.

THE PROBLEM

"I try to hit the ball straight, but it keeps going to the right."

Are you going crazy knowing that whenever you get your opponent out of position and try to pass him down the line, you proceed to pull the ball cross-court, right to him? Well, your dilemma is the same as it was on the forehand side: your swing is traveling around on a horizontal plane —like a hula-hoop—rather than out toward your intended target area.

REASONS:

Instead of having a vertical stroking plane, you are pulling off toward a horizontal plane and creating forces that require difficult manipulations to control. One of the following may be the cause of your problem:

A. You may be stepping across to the right of your intended target line, thus opening up your body as you turn into the shot.

B. Your upper body may be opening up to the shot too early and continuing to rotate horizontally. The result is the "Humble Harv" type of follow-through [3-26], seen in clubs around the world.

C. Perhaps because you are eager to see what your opponent is going to do with your shot, you may be pulling your head up before impact, which helps initiate a horizontal force.

D. Your hips may simply be rotating around on a horizontal plane.

E. Your upper arm may be stopping just before impact, forcing the racket head to roll across to the right.

F. You may be one of those players I often meet who have crummy backhands and have tried to follow the advice that they should "swing with a frisbee-toss motion." This effort, unfortunately, has turned them into wristy, inconsistent hitters who slap at the ball with a flat swing.

[3-26]

CURES:

A. One way to start eliminating horizontal forces is to step out toward your intended target area or even toward the left net post.

B. When you go out to meet the ball (swinging on a low-to-high path), stop your belly button just before impact, when it is facing the side fence [3-27]; this will prevent your right side from pulling across and will keep you from throwing your hitting shoulder around on the follow-through. Visualize the belly button as a third eye that sees the blur of the racket as it comes through the hitting zone.

C. Be patient and work hard to keep your head down, in a fixed position, through impact. Take an imaginary swing and notice how difficult it is to rotate the shoulders around to the right when you're looking down at the contact point.

D. Snap your hips hard into the shot, but stop the rotation of the right hip just before impact. This (1) keeps you from spinning around at the hips and cutting across the ball, and (2) helps turn the hitting arm into a cracking whip by stopping the right side of the body and transferring power up through the upper body and out to the racket.

E. Make sure that the upper arm continues toward the sky after impact so the energy flows out to your target area, not to the side court. Visualize an "air-the-armpit" finish, with your hitting arm extended upward, and it will help keep your racket going out in line with your intended target. Even when you're playing, occasionally freeze on the follow-through and check to see if you're doing it right.

▶ Another way to help groove this desired follow-through is to mark a fence (or a wall at home) at the point where you want to finish with the hitting hand. Then practice going to this mark with your hand as you swing [3-28].

▶ As an added kinesthetic reminder to keep from pulling across, remember that your hitting knuckles are your control system on the backhand, duplicating the palm's function on the forehand. As you turn into the shot, you might want to remind yourself, "Knuckles to the sky on the follow-through."

THE PROBLEM

"I usually feel cramped as I go to hit my backhand."

REASONS:

Basically, you're contacting the ball too close to your body; instead of playing the ball, you're letting the ball play you. Here are some of the reasons this happens to so many club players:

A. You may be forgetting that backhands (especially when you're trying to hit with topspin) must be contacted farther out in front of the body than forehands because the hitting shoulder is much closer to the net.

B. Much of your trouble could actually stem from a fearful mental attitude about the backhand. If you lack confidence on this side, you'll tend to hesitate about going after the ball and contacting it as early as you can.

C. You may be lazy with your footwork as you close in on the ball, failing to adjust your feet properly when you position yourself to swing.

D. You could be waiting too long to start your backswing, and as a result, you are rushing to complete your swing, which usually results in wrist layback —and a backswing that is too long. Just as on the forehand, if you are not careful when the arm decelerates at the end of your backswing, the racket will continue to accelerate and thus go out of synch with your body as you rotate into the shot.

CURES:

A. Get into position so you can contact the ball comfortably out in front of your body toward the net—as far in front as you can manage while still maintaining your balance. Your hitting elbow should be about a racket's-face width away from your body at impact, so measure that distance against a fence [3-29] and practice contacting a ball wedged in the fence at your ideal impact point. Try to retain that feeling of where the ball should be contacted when you go to play, and don't let it get closer to your body.

B. Since fear and hesitation undermine so many promising backhands, think aggressively when you see the ball coming to this side—and meanwhile, go to work on the stroking technique that will back up this confidence. Another key ingredient here is to

[3-29]

trust your instincts. Our research has shown that most people know where the ball is going, yet very often they simply remain rooted in their ready position, apparently waiting to reconfirm where the ball is actually going to land.

C. Use my coin drill [3-30] to practice what it means to use little shuffle steps to get into the best possible position to swing. Also practice arriving at your hitting position so early that you can literally swing in slow motion as you go out to meet the ball. This will help emphasize the footwork necessary to get you to the ball with time enough to be able to swing in slow motion, if you wanted.

D. Whenever possible, move quickly into your hitting position and rotate your hitting shoulder away from the ball well before it hits the court. This will give you the necessary time to fix your racket on the loop swing before letting it drop, thus absorbing the effects of deceleration-acceleration. Then step into the ball and start your forward swing early enough to meet the ball comfortably out in front of your body with an extended hitting arm. In fact, even as you start your backswing, think, "Way out in front." Pretty soon you'll be saying, "Hot dog! It's a backhand."

[3-30]

THE PROBLEM

"I can't seem to hit the ball with topspin."

REASONS:

A. Your racket face may be too high on the backswing, failing to drop lower than the intended point of contact so you can bring it on a low-to-high path against the ball and thereby impart topspin rotation.

▶ On the backhand side especially, you are very likely playing with stepladder legs, trying to impart topspin by simply dropping the racket head low and then swinging up through the ball with insufficient knee bend [3-31]. You can get away without much knee bend on the forehand, but not on the backhand.

B. You may be late as you go to hit the ball, which forces you to make unfortunate adjustments in your swing and dictates hitting level or with underspin.

For example, as your opponent's shot approaches, you may be failing to rotate your hitting shoulder away from the ball quickly enough or far enough. This causes you to compensate by sticking out your elbow, first on the backswing [3-32], and

then again as you come into the ball — with the result that you either underspin the shot or punch it with a horizontal stroke.

CURES:

A. In order to hit a topspin backhand, you must bend your knees enough to allow the racket head to drop well below the intended point of contact. But also, for topspin to work, the racket head must remain perpendicular to the ground and be firmly locked in at impact. This means that even against a ball that you plan to contact at about waist level, you must lower your hitting hand and the racket face down to about midthigh level in order to impart good topspin. The lower you can get, the easier (and more possible) it is to hit with topspin.

▶ Try my sit-and-hit chair drll [3-33 through 3-35] to understand how you must bend your knees to hit a topspin backhand against a waist-high ball. Stand in front of a chair and take practice swings, making sure that your rear end touches the seat on the

[3-31]

[3-32]

backswing as you go out to hit an imaginary ball (or one tossed by a friend). Touching the chair will remind you just how much knee bend is required and will give you a good idea of why your quadriceps need to be in good shape to hit with topspin.

Anatomically, on the forehand side you can stand relatively straight and still have a vertical racket face at impact. But on the backhand it won't work to stand stiff-kneed and simply drop the racket face low by loosening the wrist, hoping that your hitting arm can save the day by placing the racket in a vertical position to impart topspin. This either forces a distorted wrist position to effect a vertical racket face or produces a scooping motion (as you can see in 3-31), which yields weak, misdirected shots.

B. Learn to contact the ball comfortably out in front of your body so you're free to lift *forward and upward* into the ball. In practice, as a friend or a ball machine feeds you balls to hit at the baseline, break ingrained habits by forcing yourself to be too early. Try to exaggerate; get the feeling that you're almost falling forward because you're so far out in front. You'll very likely be right on target. Remember: if you're late on the forehand side, you can still whip the racket around and impart some topspin with sharp, low-to-high wrist action. But if you're late on the backhand, you usually have no choice but to hit a defensive return, either punched or with underspin.

THE PROBLEM

"My underspin shots keep going into the net."

[3-37]
[3-38]

REASON:

Since underspin is imparted with a high-to-low stroking motion against the back of the ball, players often make the mistake of chopping down at the ball, like lumberjacks hacking into a tree. This simply sends the ball right into the net, unless you compensate by having a severely opened (beveled) racket face at impact, which in turn undermines consistency.

CURE:

The key is to make sure that your racket face is nearly vertical as it travels through the hitting zone. So, while you must come into the ball with a high-to-low motion in order to impart underspin, strive to finish with a relatively high follow-through. You can't guide the ball safely over the net after hitting it, but this effort to take the racket quickly back up after impact will complete the desired inverted-bow stroking motion, as shown in the photographs [3-36 through 3-38].

[3-36]

THE PROBLEM

"My underspin shots are floating long."

How many times have you tilted your racket face back and tried desperately to hit the ball hard with underspin by "slicing" under the ball? How many times have you then walked out the gate, looked for the ball, and come back in to play the next point? Plenty, I'll bet, if you've listened to the myths about hitting underspin.

REASON:

You've heard that you should get your racket face *under* the ball, so you give it this look [3-39], and as a result your racket face is opened way too much at impact. Given this flaw, the harder you try to hit the ball with underspin, the more often it will go over the net and out, since it doesn't have topspin rotation helping to bring it down early.

CURE:

Instead of thinking that the racket must come under, or slice under, the ball to impart underspin—which is a myth—learn to have the racket face almost vertical at impact and concentrate on your high-to-low motion into the ball. This motion is what actually produces underspin. In fact, if your racket face is consistently tilted or laid back more than about ten degrees—a very small amount—hitting errors usually increase by a great number. The reason is that for every extra degree that you lay the racket back, you must increase the angle at which you swing down accordingly. These are difficult calculations to make from one hit to the next, especially under pressure.

A contributing problem here may be the fact that you are trying to drive your underspin backhand from baseline to baseline, instead of just playing it back safely as a purely defensive shot.

THE PROBLEM

"I hit with two hands, but I can't seem to generate much power."

Thousands of club players have converted to a two-handed backhand in recent years, inspired by all the great two-handers they've seen on the pro tour. I've long advocated the traditional one-handed backhand, but I'm also comfortable teaching people to play with two hands — provided that they understand that it requires a more supple upper body and good balance to develop a strong two-handed shot.

REASONS:

A. Like most two-handed players, you may be getting into trouble by simply taking the racket back with arm action rather than using a body coil. At best, you end up "arming" the ball over the net.

B. You could be too rigid in the upper body, swinging with tight shoulders while trying to apply an equal amount of force with both arms.

C. You may be holding an Eastern forehand grip with your regular hitting hand. This limits how far out you can go to contact the ball and makes it more comfortable to hit closer to your body, which defeats the kind of backhand you're seeking.

D. Like many two-handed players, you may have a tendency to rest your elbows against your body as you hit.

E. You may have lazy footwork, which often prevents you from having both feet well grounded and your body balanced as you go to hit.

F. You may not be utilizing the power in your lower body by lifting up into the shot.

CURES:

A. Remember, the body can uncoil into the shot and supply power only if it has been previously coiled. So your shoulders should make a good turn away from the baseline, allowing you to rotate into the shot with good hip action [3-40]. Then you must stop your front shoulder rotation just before impact so the racket head — as the last segment of the kinetic-energy chain — can go through the hitting zone faster.

B. Although your arms are moving as a unit [3-41] try to have the left hand dominate (if you are right-handed) so you're hitting more of a lefthanded forehand than a righthanded backhand. A good drill is to put the racket in just your left hand and practice hitting lefthanded forehands. Then as you play with two hands and take a loop backswing, try to feel the drop made by the left hand, for this is what helps you hit with greater power. If you're too rigid with both arms, you lose the value of a loop backswing — where gravity helps generate more racket-head speed — and it means that you're only as good as your ability to pivot and uncoil into the shot.

[3-40]

[3-41]
[3-42]

[3-43]

C. Hold an Eastern backhand grip with your normal hitting hand. This will enable you to hit with greater power, and if you eventually decide to play with one hand, you'll already have the best grip grooved.

D. Keep your arms properly extended so you can contact the ball comfortably out and away from your body [3-42] and thus gain maximum leverage.

E. Even more so than when you're hitting one-handed (where it's easier to get away with being off balance), keep both feet well grounded so that you're able to make the body uncoil properly during the swing.

F. As you uncoil into the shot, make sure that the front shoulder is leading the way out toward your intended target area and that your front hip is lifting up at the same angle as your swing [3-43].

51

THE PROBLEM

"I can't get enough power on my shots—and still keep the ball in play."

REASONS:

A. You may be relying on your hitting arm for power, rather than on your body. Hitting "all arm" usually makes the ball go short, unless your racket face is turned up at impact.

B. You may be contacting the ball too close to your body.

C. You may have weak extensor muscles in the hitting arm. This can cost you racket-head control as the match progresses and may prevent you from maintaining a firm wrist and an extended hitting arm through impact, both of which are vital for a strong backhand.

D. You may be hitting the ball with underspin rather than topspin.

CURES:

A. Many club players undermine their backhands by placing too much faith in their racket arm's action. Instead of simply taking the racket back fast and trying to whip through the shot, you should work on these techniques:

▶ Coil your upper body on the backswing so you can unwind into the shot (imagine an X on the back of your hitting shoulder that stays in sight of your opponent, like the one I'm wearing in 3-44). By turning your hitting shoulder back to initiate the backswing pivot—rotating your body away from the ball—you set everything up, and you can now uncoil into the ball with your knees, hips, and shoulders.

▶ Unwind into the shot until just before impact, when you want to gain stopping power from the upper body. If you can stop your front shoulder just before impact, the arm will snap out and whip the racket faster into the ball. Also think about having your belly button stop just before impact, which will help the racket travel even faster. Although Eliot Teltscher, for example, is one of the lightest players on the tour, he gains tremendous force by coiling his upper body as he sets up for the shot, then abruptly stopping the rotation of his midsection in the middle of the forward swing. That sudden deceleration of

[3-44]

his uncoiling trunk actually accelerates his swinging arm. By the time the strings hit the ball, Teltscher's racket head is moving at tremendous speed. And that speed comes from the natural whipping motion generated by his upper body's sudden stop. Ivan Lendl hits much the same way.

▶ Step toward the ball and bend your knees so you can transfer your weight into the shot as you lift upward and forward, utilizing the power in your thighs as you drive the ball with topspin. My sit-and-hit chair drill (page 46) will help you groove this bending and lifting motion as you step into the ball.

▶ Since your body obviously has much more mass than your racket arm, rely on the arm to trace a perfect stroke pattern as you use the body to generate all the power you need. And instead of horsing around with the racket head, keep it in a fixed position while uncoiling your body into the shot. As you make the transition to greater body coil, practice coiling more than seems natural. Typically, only by exaggerating desired movements can we overcome ingrained bad habits. It can also be helpful to swing without a racket in order to better sense what it means to coil the body. Many of my students *think* they're coiling, only to realize they're simply taking the racket back a little farther than normal.

B. In order to hit with power and topspin, learn to contact the ball comfortably in front of your body so you're free to be aggressive on the shot. The earlier you can hit the ball—while staying in balance and in control—the greater your potential power. Why? Because it means that you are transferring your weight forward into the shot while lengthening the radius of your stroke, which increases your racket-head speed. When you hit the ball late—and too close to your body—the racket head is unable to generate significant speed before impact; you're not as able to capitalize on that long lever attached to your hitting hand.

Another advantage of hitting off your front foot and taking the ball early is that you can play offensively from the baseline. When you see that your deep drive is going to put your opponent on the defensive, your momentum is already going toward the net if you decide to attack.

C. Strengthen your extensor muscles with the exercises described on pages 30–31.

D. Learn to hit with topspin so you can slug the ball hard and still bring it down inside your opponent's baseline. Hitting with the same power *and* safety isn't possible when you opt for underspin or try to hit "net-skimmers" with a level swing.

THE PROBLEM

"When I try to hit the ball hard, it usually goes long."

REASONS:

If you're the type of player who loves to slug the ball, but it rarely stays inside the county, the underlying problem is either or both of the following:

A. Hitting the ball too hard with insufficient topspin.

B. A racket face that is beveled or turned up at impact [3-45].

CURES:

A. When it comes to ball rotation and backhand drives, there are two considerations:

▶ If you presently hit the ball hard and flat, with little trajectory over the net, you must learn to impart topspin to the ball. This will allow you to swing hard while elevating the ball safely over the net, confident that your shots should generally land inside your opponent's baseline.

▶ If you already have a good low-to-high swing for topspin and you've determined that the racket face is vertical at impact, then you must learn to swing on a steeper upward angle.

For example, if you want to apply minimal topspin but elevate the ball safely over the net with moderate speed, you must swing upward at about a 20-degree angle. If you want to hit a good topspin drive, the racket must travel at a steeper upward angle—about 45 degrees. At this angle, the ball will have increased topspin and a sharper arc as it clears the net. Then, if you're thinking, "I'm angry all the time when I'm playing—I want to hit as hard as I can," you had better learn to swing to the sky at about an 80-degree angle. Now get out on the court and practice hitting the ball hard, trying to sense just how steep an angle the racket must travel at on a low-to-high path as it comes into the ball.

B. Play with a fixed wrist position and a firm forearm to help guarantee a vertical racket face at im-

[3-45]

pact, one hit after another. This frees you to swing aggressively, knowing that when it comes to depth you have to worry only about the upward angle of your swing.

CHAPTER 4

The Serve

THE PROBLEM

"My hard serves keep going into the net."

REASONS:

A. You may be trying to hit down on the ball by snapping down with the racket. Perhaps you've been told to "stretch up so you can hit down on the serve," but this advice ignores the fact that not even a seven-footer can swing down at impact and expect the ball to clear the net. The net is simply too high a barrier, and the force of gravity acting on the ball too strong, to allow this.

B. You may be looking at your intended target area on the court just before starting your service motion. In order to see that target, you must actually look through the net, thus creating the wrong imagery as you prepare to hit and perhaps causing you to pull the ball down into the net. Research has shown that muscle movement is often led by the eyes.

C. You may be dropping your chin before impact [4-1]. This creates a strong downward force by the body as your racket comes into the hitting zone,

[4-1]

pulling the racket face down. Any downward force before you strike the ball detracts from the desired position of the racket face at impact, as indicated by the ball's placement at the top of the strings in the photograph.

D. The ball toss may be too far out in front of your body (seldom a problem with club players).

E. You may be holding an Eastern forehand grip as you serve, thus severely restricting the amount of spin you can impart to the ball. By keeping you from having a pronating forearm action in the hitting zone, the Eastern grip limits you to a hard but unpredictable flat serve, which has only a thin safety margin over the net because the ball is not arcing with topspin.

CURES:

A. Instead of thinking that you can slug the ball down, visualize yourself as a midget hitting "up and out" at the ball and letting spin and gravity bring it down. It responds to the laws of physics like any other object. At the impact point, the racket face is usually vertical and extended [4-2], and you should be thinking about hitting across a tabletop, not down.

B. Just as on your groundstrokes, try to visualize a target area above the net instead of inside your opponent's service box. When you consciously try to hit your serve out through this "air target," you may be surprised to realize just how much you have to swing *up* on the ball to gain real depth.

C. Here are some tips to help you keep your chin up and your eyes on the ball through contact:

▶ Consciously think about keeping the front shoulder up and keeping the upper body from collapsing before impact.

▶ Think to yourself, "Stretch the Adam's apple" or "Chin to the top of the fence" [4-3] as you swing.

▶ Look beyond the ball toss—perhaps to the lights above the court fence [4-4]—as a way to keep your head and upper body up through impact. Most people are so eager to see where their serve is going that they pull down too early.

▶ Try to watch the blur of the racket face as it travels through the contact zone. Roscoe Tanner, one of the great servers of all time, once said, "I try to keep my head up as much as possible and follow the ball with my eyes even as I hit it."

D. Toss the ball closer to your body and not so far toward the net.

E. Move your palm toward the top of the racket grip in order to serve with a Continental grip— halfway between the Eastern forehand and the Eastern backhand. By allowing much greater forearm flexibility as your racket sweeps through the impact zone, the Continental enables you to hit serves with spin, power, and control while at the same time placing less stress on the arm.

THE PROBLEM

"My first serves are consistently too long."

While it's true that if you're going to make service errors, you should be long rather than short, what about those times during a match when you can't seem to bring the ball in, especially on the first serve?

REASONS:

A. You may be contacting the ball too much above or behind your body as the result of a bad toss [4-5]. This causes the racket face to be open or pointed toward the sky at impact, which sends the ball long.

B. The ball toss may be correct — out ahead of your body, off the hitting shoulder — but your racket head may be laid back at impact anyway.

C. You may be hitting the ball hard but with insufficient topspin to bring it into play.

CURES:

A. Toss the ball farther out in front of your body [4-6], but keep thinking "upward and out" as you

hit. Also, keep in mind that you're not required to swing at a lousy toss, so if it's off course, let the ball fall and try again.

B. Remember, the racket face must be vertical at impact in order for you to hit the ball hard and impart the spin that will bring the ball down inside the service line.

C. Instead of hitting the ball hard and flat — which forces you to skim the net and can bring grief on those days when your timing is not absolutely perfect — learn to impart topspin rotation to the ball.

Start by throwing a lower toss than you're used to so your racket can strike the ball on a low-to-high diagonal path [4-7] rather than at the peak of your reach, which is where you should contact flat and slice serves. A topspin serve requires that you have a low enough toss that you can contact the ball at *its* peak while the racket is still rising.

A second key is to toss the ball comfortably out in front of your body so you're free to come forward as you hit up, with the racket strings straight up and down at impact. Think about making the racket

[4-5]

[4-6]

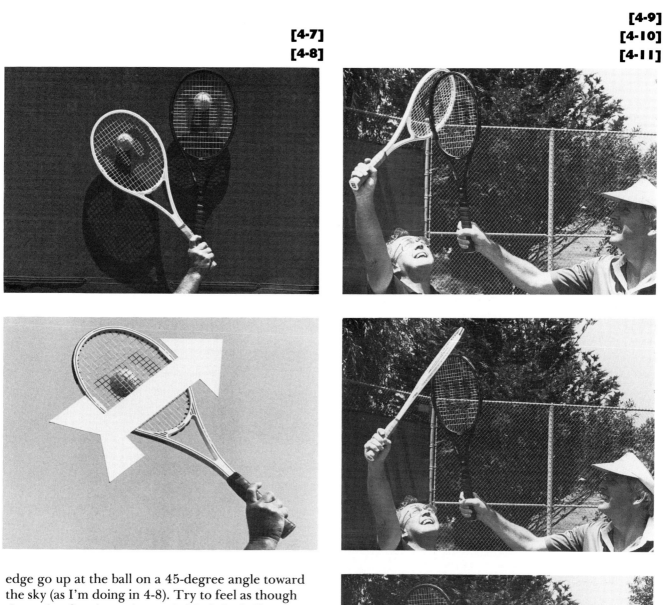

edge go up at the ball on a 45-degree angle toward the sky (as I'm doing in 4-8). Try to feel as though the racket face is coming up behind the ball and rolling over its top right side. This is not what physically happens, of course, since the ball leaves the racket strings instantly at impact, but that's the imagery I seek. You can achieve the same feeling by bringing your racket face up and over a friend's racket [4-9 through 4-11]. Again, the racket doesn't really behave as shown in 4-10 when you actually hit the ball.

Also remember that in order to swing just as hard as you do now but make the ball fall shorter you must increase topspin rotation by hitting up against the ball at a steeper upward angle.

THE PROBLEM

"I have a good high toss but a weak serve."

If you tend to regard the service motion as an intricate beast that requires a lot of preparation time, it may seem important to you to toss the ball high and give yourself plenty of time to swing. In reality, though, tossing the ball beyond the peak of your racket reach simply gives you more time to hit a lousy serve.

REASONS:

A. A high toss beyond your outstretched racket actually gives you much less time to hit an accurate serve than a good low toss — ideally, one that dictates a continuous service motion and allows you to meet the ball with your racket arm comfortably extended [4-12].

In fact, our high-speed photography of ball tosses showed that servers get almost 30 times more hitting time off a low toss than off a high one. When you can strike the ball as it is reaching its apex, at its peak, or as it begins to drop, you have a virtually motionless target that seems to be hanging from a string. By contrast, a high toss, pulled down by gravity, falls rapidly through the hitting zone and requires you to judge the flight of the ball much more precisely. Having to make these calculations greatly increases the chances of your mistiming the hit and having something go wrong with your accuracy, especially under pressure and on windy days.

B. Tossing the ball higher than necessary forces you to wait for it to drop, which means that somewhere during the swing you must slow down or even

[4-12]

[4-13]

stop your racket and body movements. This disrupts the smooth, continuous uncoiling motion you should be seeking.

To check whether your toss is too high (in relation to the service motion I advocate in this chapter), release the ball as you would for a regular serve and take a *continuous* swing, not pausing at all to adjust for the height of your toss. If you miss the ball completely, then your toss is too high and you must lower it while going to work on your swing. Missing the ball like this should also bring home just how much braking action you've built into your service motion.

CURES:

A. You can lay the foundation for a great serve by simply lifting the ball up about 20 to 24 inches out of your tossing hand—less than the length of your racket. This will give you sufficient time to complete your swing, provided that your tossing motion and the swing itself follow my guidelines.

B. Stand against a fence or wall and determine where you can comfortably contact the ball by extending your racket up and out; then mark that spot and practice making your toss go to this mark **[4-13]**. Unless you grow or shrink an inch or two, that should be your target height for the toss on flat and slice serves for the rest of your life. The toss for top-spin serves will be even lower than that, by about three or four inches (as we saw in 4-7).

THE PROBLEM

"My toss is inconsistent."

An unreliable toss that travels to a slightly different location every time undermines the best of service motions by forcing subtle little adjustments on every swing. Many club players perpetuate this problem by making these adjustments on one serve after another instead of mastering one consistent toss to accommodate a perfect service motion.

REASONS:

A. You may be spreading your arms apart too early as you begin to take the racket back [4-14]. This means that the tossing hand is going out toward your opponent and then up to release the ball, which forces you to make a dangerously high toss in order to have enough time to complete your stroke.

B. You may have excessive upper-body coil on the backswing. I place such an importance on shoulder rotation that some of my students think, "If a little body coil is good, a big coil ought to be great." So

they make too much of a turn, which forces the tossing hand back too far and leads to wild tosses.

C. You may be contracting too many muscles as you hold the ball and release the toss.

D. Your toss may be too high and thus more difficult to control.

CURES:

A. Initiate the service motion by taking both hands back together until the tossing arm is just about parallel to the baseline and the hand passes the belly button [4-15 through 4-17]. Then, with an arching motion of the tossing hand, release the ball up, out, and away from your body [4-18] to the peak of your reach, or slightly lower if you are hitting a topspin serve. By having both hands work together in a synchronized action, rather than going their separate ways at the beginning of your motion, you can throw a nice low toss and still have plenty of time to swing.

(continued)

[4-14]

[4-15]
[4-16]

[4-17]
[4-18]

Here's a drill that will help you develop the proper swinging rhythm, learn to release the ball on a nice arc, and lower your toss for a better serve. Stand as though you're preparing to serve, but with a ball in *each* hand as you look toward your opponent [4-19]. Now take your backswing, thinking "turn" at this point, not "throw," as you rotate the upper body and bring both hands back together [4-20]. Then make the balls follow each other upward. Release the tossing ball as your hands get to about shoulder height, and try to hit it with the second ball [4-21 and 4-22]. You won't have to rush your swing, even if your toss is only six or eight inches out of your hand. Keep this imagery in mind when you serve with a racket in your hand.

B. To prevent excessive body coil, the tossing arm should come back no farther than parallel to the baseline before going up to release the ball. Not only is bringing the arm back beyond that point unnecessary, it also undermines a consistent toss by forcing a longer upward arc and making the toss more difficult to control.

[4-20]

C. Hold the ball sideways or with the palm facing down as you take the tossing hand back and release the ball. Notice that the more the palm is facing toward the sky, the greater the tension in your hand, wrist, and forearm and the more the muscles have to work—leading to difficulties as you try to groove a nice easy tossing motion.

D. Lower your toss to an ideal target area that is at or near the peak of your racket's reach (based upon the type of serve you want to hit) and out in front of your body, off the hitting shoulder. Mark that point against a fence or wall (as described on page 61) and practice tossing the ball to this point.

THE PROBLEM

"I have a classic serving pose — the kind you see on trophies — but I can't beat my aunt Bertha."

REASON:

If you strike the famous trophy pose [4-23], by forming a beautiful straight line from your outstretched tossing hand down to the bent hitting arm behind your back, *that's* the reason for your problem. "How can that be when I look terrific?" you're thinking. Well, dropping the hitting elbow too low on the backswing momentarily halts the continuous motion that is crucial to a powerful serve. And when the racket head stops, you might as well be starting at the point where you've paused.

CURES:

You may have to address several flaws as you work to correct the trophy look.

▶ As much as possible, keep your movements on a horizontal plane until you stretch to hit up and out at the ball, for it's the horizontal trunk rotation that sets up the action you want with the hitting arm. So:

▶ Initiate your backswing by turning away from your opponent with a horizontal pivot of both shoulders. As a drill, face the net and stand flat-

[4-23]

footed when you serve. This forces you to rotate at the shoulders in order to hit the ball hard.

► Instead of rocking back or using an exaggerated up-and-down action of the legs, keep your weight evenly distributed as you turn on a horizontal plane.

► Keep the front shoulder up and the hitting elbow high as you take the backswing. Here's a good drill that serves several purposes at once. Wedge a ball in the back fence at shoulder level (indicated by the X in 4-24) and then step away until you can nearly touch the ball with your racket when the arm is held outstretched on the backswing. Now go through the serve motion, paying close attention to the moment when your racket is pointed toward that ball in the fence. That's your cue to start turning your knees for-

ward, which automatically initiates a forward weight shift, followed by an unwinding into the shot as you let the hitting elbow collapse to initiate the loop.

► Purge yourself of any notion that you must "scratch the back" in order to serve the ball hard. As I point out on pages 70–71, this "back-scratching" effort undermines what you're trying to achieve. Instead, let the racket fall naturally toward your back as your body uncoils into the shot, and the desired loop will occur automatically.

► Lower your toss so you're forced to maintain a quick, easy shoulder roll and a continuous motion as you swing. A high toss—beyond your outstretched racket—could be resulting in the "trophy" look as you wait for the ball to drop, poised with your hitting arm drawn back and the elbow lowered.

THE PROBLEM

"I have trouble coordinating my swing with the toss."

REASONS:

A. Your toss may be too high and inconsistent. When club players especially have an unnecessarily high toss, they tend to add destructive extra movements to their swing, which make it more difficult to contact the toss properly.

B. You may have too many excess movements in your overall serving motion. While it's true that the serve is not simple physiologically, I see people everywhere going through unbelievable gyrations that leave them out of control and make the serve unnecessarily difficult. Some service motions are so intricate and complex that I'm amazed that the person can actually remember the movements from one serve to the next.

C. You may be taking the racket back too far on the backswing. Contrary to what most people think, the length of the backswing is not the key to gaining more power. In fact, stretching the hitting arm out to gain more length limits your potential power — and consistency — by creating a windup that keeps you from uncoiling properly into the shot.

CURES:

A. Lower your toss to the peak of your racket reach and then practice making the ball go to this ideal striking point on one toss after another (as discussed on page 61). This low toss will, in turn, emphasize the importance of developing a smooth, continuous service motion that will allow you to strike the ball at or near its peak. Also use my two-ball drill (page 64) to coordinate a lower toss with your service motion (again, assuming that you're taking both arms back together before releasing the toss).

B. Strive to decrease the number of joint segments that are involved in your motion, rather than adding fancy new movements. Concentrate on developing a nice easy shoulder roll as you work to eliminate the hitches and jerky movements that rob you of rhythm and potential power. You don't need all of these bizarre movements in order to hit a great serve.

When you first try to strip away this excess motion, you may feel a bit strange and uncomfortable — skeptical about whether you're now doing enough to hit the ball hard — but rest assured that you're making the right transition.

C. Maintain good upper-body rotation, but shorten your motion so the hitting arm basically stays on the belly-button side of your body. My earlier drill against the fence (page 67) can help you learn just how far you should take the racket back before turning up and into the shot. Here again, you may doubt that such a short swing can generate sufficient power, but it actually puts the body into perfect synchronization with the racket and your toss.

THE PROBLEM

"My hitting arm seems to be too stiff as I swing."

Everything can fall nicely into place when the hitting arm remains loosey-goosey from the backswing through impact. But if you indeed serve with a stiff arm, or with one that tightens up as you progress through the motion, then you are undermining your potential to hit the ball hard. Even if you block your front shoulder properly just before impact, a tight racket arm can't act as a whip to transfer energy out through the racket.

REASONS:

A. Your toss may be too high, causing the racket arm to pause or stiffen up as you wait for the ball to come down.

B. Your hitting palm may be facing UP on the backswing. This automatically prevents the looping action that generates power and rhythm.

C. You may be making an intentional effort to force the racket down into a "back-scratch" position, which usually makes the wrong muscles contract and promotes rigidity.

D. You could be consciously trying to "slug" the ball, which inhibits the looseness you ought to be seeking.

CURES:

A. Lower your toss to a point that dictates a continuous serving motion. This low toss means that you can't afford to let the racket arm pause, or you'll whiff the shot.

B. Make sure that the hitting palm is facing DOWN as you take the racket back in synchronization with the tossing hand [4-25].

C. Some people find it helpful to think of the hitting arm as a rope—with a racket attached—as they

[4-25]

pivot into the shot and let the racket complete a natural looping action behind their backs.

D. Instead of straining to hit the ball hard, assume a relaxed stance as you begin the serve; this will aid an easy, rhythmical hitting motion. Just before starting your backswing, consciously relax your shoulders and tell yourself to "let the arm go spaghetti" as a reminder to keep the hitting arm loose and lanky. Then let everything flow.

THE PROBLEM

"I can't seem to achieve a loop backswing."

[4-27]
[4-28]

A looping action by the racket as it falls behind your body on the backswing helps generate considerable racket-head speed. If this loop is missing, you lose your potential to hit the ball consistently hard.

REASONS:

A. Your hitting palm may be facing UP on the backswing. Turning the palm up like this as you take the racket back [4-26] makes the looping action you're seeking anatomically impossible.

B. You may be consciously trying to "scratch the back." You'll often hear or read the advice to "scratch your back with your racket" to achieve a desired loop on the backswing. But this deliberate effort to make the racket touch the back [4-27] not only looks funny, it also keeps you from achieving the smooth, rhythmic flow that can generate tremendous power from the service motion. In fact, the closer you come to actually "scratching" your back,

[4-26]

the weaker your serve will be, for this effort momentarily stops the body's rotation and eliminates the racket speed you want to be generating at that point.

CURES:

A. Make sure that the hitting palm is facing *down* on the backswing [4-28] so the racket face is also facing down as you turn into the ball. This sets up the racket's looping action behind your back.

B. The loop will occur automatically if you can swing with a loose, relaxed hitting arm and rely on a continuous shoulder action as the body unwinds into the shot. Start this desired sequence by taking the hitting arm back horizontally and then letting it fall freely *toward* your back as you turn into the toss [4-29 and 4-30]. The body's uncoiling action—starting at the knees—will dictate what happens next. When you are serving correctly, the force of your rotating upper body is so great that it actually throws the racket out and away from the body [4-31]. Strive for a back-scratching *feeling,* but not an actuality.

THE PROBLEM

"My serves are in play but landing too short."

Your problem may not be so much catching the net as having your serves consistently land short, giving your opponent easier balls to return and keeping you on the defensive.

REASON:

You're trying to hit down on the ball.

CURES:

▶ Review the coaching suggestions in the related tip on pages 56–57, since they deal with the same potential flaws in your serving technique. Several key reminders: keep your chin up at impact [4-32], contact the ball comfortably out in front of your hitting shoulder, and concentrate on hitting the ball out through your target window *above* the net. This will greatly improve your odds of hitting the ball safely over the net AND deep.

▶ Establish a psychological pattern of always wanting to serve the ball deep—either good or beyond the service line—and never into the net. Keeping your opponent pinned deep with serves just inside the service line will prevent him from taking the net and will give you more time to react to his return. Also, your opponent may play some serves that are actually out; he can't give you that break if the ball goes into the net.

[4-32]

THE PROBLEM

"I'm 'scratching my back' perfectly, but I still can't get any power."

REASONS:

When you try to "scratch the back" by pushing your racket down on the backswing [4-33], you may think you're setting up to hit a gigantic serve. Unfortunately, you don't have a prayer.

A. One reason is that you've destroyed the energy-producing chain, which should start at your knees, continue up through your trunk, and then flow out to your forearm and the racket as you uncoil into the shot with a continuous arm and upper-body motion. The "scratch the back" effort creates a braking action, nullifying the buildup of racket-head speed that is necessary to hit the ball hard, and forces you to rely on the power in your arm.

B. When you "scratch the back," the flexor muscles in your hitting arm contract, which in turn inhibits you from snapping the forearm into the shot as the racket comes through the hitting zone. Our comparative research studies showed that there's little contraction of the flexors by top servers.

CURES:

A and B. Instead of straining to "scratch the back," allow the racket to fall naturally toward your back as you turn into the shot [4-34]. The force of your rotating body will make the racket loop automatically, without any conscious effort on your part, provided the hitting palm is down on your backswing. Many pros look as if they're "scratching the back" when viewed from the stands, but not when we film them from above. We find that the harder they serve, the farther the racket comes away from the body on the backswing loop and as it starts up toward the toss. The weaker the server, the closer the racket comes to the body. Students at my tennis college are stunned to see these contrasts when they view our high-speed aerial footage.

[4-33]

[4-34]

THE PROBLEM

"The racket keeps hitting my legs on the follow-through."

You may chuckle if this isn't one of your problems [4-35], but it's a painful price many players think they have to pay as they try to become famous in this game. You can usually spot these people by the hash-marks on their legs.

REASONS:

You may think that power on the serve comes from swinging hard and having an explosive wrist snap just before impact. So you're tossing the ball straight out in front of your body, pushing your hitting arm at it, and trying to have the hitting hand come straight through toward your opponent as the wrist

is snapping. As a result, you have a cream-puff serve and bruised legs.

By focusing on a straight-ahead wrist snap, you are overlooking the secret to power on the serve: mastering the kinetic-energy chain, which culminates in a pronating action by the forearm just before impact. Our research shows that the wrist itself is relatively inactive at impact and that the greatest amount of force is generated by forearm pronation—in which the hitting palm rotates downward and out [4-36 through 4-38]. When this pronating action is missing, you lose the power potential in your serve.

(continued)

[4-35]

[4-36]

[4-37]

[4-38]

CURES:

Start tossing the ball farther out to the side, off your hitting shoulder and comfortably out in front of your body, so you're free to swing up and out at the ball. Also make sure that you are rotating your upper body on the backswing so you can uncoil into the shot with a loose hitting arm.

Instead of thinking that you must hit straight through the ball with a big wrist snap, concentrate on forearm pronation as your racket face travels up to the toss and out across the ball, to the right of your head (as I'm doing in 4-36 through 4-38). Think "Snap the forearm" as you go up to strike the ball, and maintain a loose, whipping action by the racket arm. By turning into the shot properly and allowing the loop to occur naturally, you generate a horizontal force that throws the racket away from the body

as you stretch toward the toss. Keep that energy flowing by having your hitting arm move *upward and outward,* with the forearm pronating under and away from the impact point—out to the right of your target line, not straight ahead.

▶ To sense just what it means to have forearm pronation, stand and hold a ball in your tossing hand, with nothing in your racket hand. Now just throw the ball up about ten inches and hit it with your open hitting palm as the forearm rotates down and away in the impact zone. Next, bring both arms back together as you would on the serve and again throw the ball up about ten inches [4-39]. Contact the ball with the hitting palm [4-40] and notice that the forearm pronates along with the hand [4-41]. This drill simulates the exact action of the palm and forearm when a racket is in that hand [4-42].

[4-39]

THE PROBLEM

"When I try to nail the ball hard, my serves go wild."

Do you sometimes feel as though you're tearing your arm out of the shoulder socket as you try to slug your first serve on a big point? And do you find that you often miss this serve, or that it rarely strikes terror into your opponent's heart? If so, you share a common frustration with millions of other players.

REASONS:

A. You may be hitting the serve hard but with insufficient ball rotation (i.e., topspin) to bring it down into the service box.

B. You may be tossing the ball straight above your head [4-43] and thus constricting your stroking motion. The forearm cannot achieve maximum speed at this point, resulting in weaker serves for most players. Some players still manage to hit the ball reasonably hard, but only by fierce recruiting of their muscles, and they tend to damage their shoulders eventually.

C. You may be recruiting the wrong muscles, tightening the hitting arm for a big, muscular effort that actually causes you to physiologically oppose your own serve. Straining to hit as hard as you can usually contracts the bicep muscle and pulls your hitting arm in toward your body, when in fact the secret is to snap the arm *out*—up and away from your body—as you go to contact the ball.

D. You may be taking too fast a backswing, forcing you to slow up or even stop your swing as you wait on the toss.

CURES:

A. Gain the ball rotation you need by getting more forearm pronation and by increasing the upward angle at which you strike the ball (see page 82). Instead of hitting forward and up on a relatively horizontal path, strike the ball with your racket head moving up on about a 45-degree angle or more. You can still swing hard, but now you'll have greater control as the ball comes in with a greater arc over the net.

B. Throw the ball farther forward off your hitting shoulder so you're free to hit up and out through the ball as you lean into the court [4-44].

C. Remember that power comes from the related efforts of your uncoiling body and a loose hitting arm—not necessarily from how strong you are or how hard you try to swing. Review the tip on page 69

[4-43]

[4-44]

for suggestions that can help you stay loose as you swing, especially at key points in a tough match.

D. Most people who try to hit hard get out of synchronization, so pay close attention to your rhythm as you swing. Never feel that you must rush your serve. Just relax and take your time; the ball isn't going anywhere until you hit it. Start slowly as you coil the body going back and strive for a continuous motion, then focus on letting the swing unwind so the racket is steadily picking up speed all the way into contact. When you take both hands back together before releasing the toss, there's plenty of time to let the swing gradually accelerate so the racket face can reach maximum speed where it is most meaningful: at impact.

THE PROBLEM

"I can't seem to hit the ball hard enough to give my opponents trouble; my last ace was in '82 — during a tornado."

REASONS:

A. Your hitting palm may be facing UP on the backswing, keeping you from having the natural looping action that generates maximum racket-head speed.

B. You may have insufficient body rotation at the beginning of the backswing. This means, for one thing, that your arms are spreading apart too early, as your tossing hand goes up to release a high toss. Such action limits upper-body rotation and sets up the famous "trophy" pose, which in turn destroys the continuous motion you should be seeking. Also, if the body doesn't coil, then it can't uncoil into the ball and contribute to your power.

C. You may be failing to block the front side of your body just before impact. The front shoulder should lead the way as you turn into the toss, but if you let this shoulder simply rotate around in a continuous motion, then the upper body can't stop just before impact and make the racket arm work as a whip. The tossing hand could be a culprit here if you simply let it travel behind you after releasing the ball [4-45]; this diverts energy away from your serve.

D. You could be pushing your forearm into the shot and not stopping the *hitting* shoulder for an instant, just before impact. As a result, you're not snapping the forearm through properly in the impact zone.

CURES:

A. Keep your hitting arm relaxed—and your hitting palm facing down—as you take the racket back, so it can make a natural looping motion when you rotate toward the ball toss.

B. Rotate your upper body away from the net as you start your backswing, at the same time bringing your hands back in tandem in order to set up a perfect ball-toss motion (see page 62). Most people think "toss" when they walk to the service line, but you can facilitate body rotation by telling yourself, "Turn the shoulders, *then* toss."

C. Learn to harness the natural whipping action created by the upper body's stopping power. The

[4-45]

fastest servers around are not necessarily the biggest, strongest players, but they gain that extra measure of power by knowing how to stop the rotation of their upper bodies milliseconds before impact. This sudden braking creates an accelerated whipping motion of the hitting arm and makes the forearm snap, allowing you to hit the ball with much more power by transferring tremendous energy out to the racket at impact.

▶ It's important here to make sure that your throwing hand is coming in against your body after

in order to deliver tremendous energy out through the racket and into your serve. Blocking the front side of the body just before impact helps stop the hitting shoulder momentarily, but you should also make a conscious effort with the shoulder itself to ensure that this is happening.

Always remember: power in tennis is related to racket-head speed at impact. So think of a flycaster or a person using a bullwhip as you visualize how kinetic energy can maximize this desired speed. Starting at the knees and working up through the hips and shoulders, uncoil your body and try to think of only one thing: transferring all this potential energy to your hitting arm. Rotate your hitting shoulder into the shot, but just before striking the ball stop this shoulder abruptly to create a whipping action of the arm. This transfers energy to the forearm just as it is pronating through at impact. The hitting shoulder on its own will then continue through on the follow-through and fall naturally. You have been building up tremendous potential energy while uncoiling into the serve — stopping each of the body segments in succession from the ground up — and now, by halting the hitting shoulder, you whip all this potential power out through the arm to the racket head. Without worrying about hitting a ball, uncoil into an imaginary serve and notice that the forearm snaps — as if you were a flycaster — when you abruptly stop the hitting shoulder.

Here's a drill to help you recognize whether you're utilizing (1) the stopping power in *both* shoulders, (2) a whipping motion with your hitting arm, and (3) forearm pronation. This drill will also help you improve these desired elements.

Start by positioning yourself just behind the baseline, with both feet facing the net. Now turn your body back, release the toss, and see how well you can hit the ball *without moving your feet*. If you can't hit the ball hard, then you lack the desired shoulder motion, and your forearm is not snapping as it should. Even standing flat-footed, you should be able to hit the ball surprisingly hard just by stopping your shoulders when they reach the baseline and by pronating the forearm as the racket travels through the hitting zone.

the toss is released and before the ball is impacted [4-46]. "That's a strange look," you say, but that's the earmark of all top servers, for this subtle action helps stop the uncoiling body and turn the hitting forearm into a whip.

▶ Keeping your chin up through impact will almost automatically stop the rotation of your front shoulder as you unwind your body into the serve.

D. Instead of letting the hitting shoulder travel through impact in one continuous motion, stop that shoulder for just an instant — slightly before impact —

THE PROBLEM

"I often choke my second serve."

REASON:

Fear could be inhibiting your serving motion, and you've resigned yourself to hitting a helium ball just to make sure it goes in.

One problem we all face with the second serve is the realization that "This ball has to go in or I lose the point." When you're afraid like this as you go to swing, the wrong muscles contract and make it even harder to hit a decent serve. Moreover, you may be making the situation worse by choosing simply to baby the ball across the net, which is the typical response in a tough situation. Unfortunately, by slowing down your swing this way you invariably hit the ball into the net, long, or right to your opponent for a put-away offensive return.

CURE:

Learn to hit with topspin so you can swing as hard as you want—whatever the pressure—and crack a second serve that's almost as fast as a good first serve. Basically, learn to hit BOTH serves with topspin, using the same service motion and simply adjusting the upward angle at which you contact the ball.

When you miss your first big bomb, don't slow up on the second attempt, and don't alter your toss; hit all-out but increase the upward angle of your stroke. This will impart greater spin for greater control. You must actually swing harder on the second serve, but the ball will come in with less speed to your opponent because the ball is depressed less and you've added more topspin rotation to force it to "bend" into the court.

Now you're thinking, "If I hit the first serve long, you want me to swing HARDER on the second serve? That ain't gonna work." Yes, this may sound illogical, but it works, because the real secret is ball rotation, not pace. The more rotation the ball has, the harder you can swing. So the solution is not to take a lot of speed off your hard first serve in order to get a high percentage of second serves in play. Keep slugging the ball hard, but learn to get topspin rotation on it. This will allow you to hit hard and still feel confident, knowing that the ball should arch safely over the net and come down into play.

By minimizing critical inhibiting factors, this ability to swing hard on the second serve and still have the ball go in should help keep you from choking.

CHAPTER 5

The Serve Return

THE PROBLEM

"I'm always late against a fast serve."

REASONS:

A. You may be standing too close to the server.

B. You may be getting too low in the ready position [5-1]. An exaggerated crouch lowers your center of gravity and makes it harder to get a fast first lateral step toward the ball.

C. You may be letting your feet fall asleep as you watch your opponent serve.

D. You may not be trying to anticipate the server's intention, and may be waiting too long to break for the ball.

E. You may not be practicing enough against hard servers. I find that people who flounder against the big hitters at their playing level tend to avoid this type of opponent around the club. So when they get into a tournament and come up against a tough server, they are tactically and psychologically ill-prepared.

CURES:

A. If necessary, move back in your waiting position until you feel comfortable about always advancing forward—on a diagonal—against as many different serves as possible. Then instead of always being forced onto the defensive, you can move more confidently toward the ball.

B. Wait for the serve in a high but comfortable body position [5-2], so your first move can be toward the ball, not upward. Research shows that when you want to break laterally or forward on a diagonal, the body makes its fastest initial movement from a high position as opposed to a crouching position. Many tournament pros mislead spectators by hunching low as they initially wait for the serve, but they stand relatively upright or even fairly erect just before the ball is actually hit. After all, most service returns in big-time tennis must be contacted at chest or shoulder level.

C. Since your ability to get a fast first step toward the ball is much more important than your actual speed of foot, make sure you're getting up on the balls of your feet as the server makes his toss, which

[5-1]

forces your weight forward and off your heels [5-3]. Yet you should also remain comfortably balanced as you await serve, so that you can move quickly with short, rapid steps either to the left or to the right.

D. You must practice anticipation and starting early against strong servers. Try these drills as a way to improve your anticipation skills and your ability to get started earlier toward the ball:

▶ Have a friend hit 20 or 30 serves, and practice guessing where the ball is going to go as soon as you see it come off the racket. At first, you may indeed be guessing, but as you learn to study a server's motion and ball toss you'll find that your original decisions are usually the most appropriate.

▶ Go into a match determined to practice anticipating your opponent's serve as early as possible — win, lose, or draw. Play an anticipation match where you try to guess where the serve is coming to and just go for it, even if you're dead wrong. Trust your initial instincts and practice breaking in one direction or the other. Don't worry about looking foolish, because you'll be quite surprised at how often your original judgments — even your guesses — are correct.

▶ Quicken your reactions and movements by trying to meet the ball 6 to 12 inches out in front of where you normally contact it. Also think about laying off those low-cal doughnuts.

▶ Starting from your usual ready position, try to go forward against every serve, no matter how fast

[5-3]

[5-2]

the ball is coming. You may be jammed by many serves or forced to hit the ball on the rise, but you should also realize just how often you actually have time to go forward and how many balls you can reach early enough to hit.

▶ Whenever possible, study your potential opponents from the sideline as they play a match. As you try to guess whether their serves are going to the left or right, you'll begin to notice how they telegraph their intentions.

E. Instead of always playing against slow- and medium-paced servers, seek out some hard hitters at your club so you'll be forced to work on your anticipation and coverage skills.

THE PROBLEM

"I get to the ball, but I tend to hit weak returns."

REASONS:

A. If making solid contact is often your problem, you could be too defensive—backing up when the serve comes instead of going forward. Edging backward like this usually causes the body to be leaning back and the racket face to be tilted back coming into impact, resulting in an ineffective service return.

B. On the forehand side, you may be tucking your elbow in against your body as you approach the ball. This not only cramps your stroke but also lays the racket head back, out of line with the incoming serve, which makes it difficult to meet the ball squarely and consistently.

C. You may be opting for a defensive approach on the backhand side by contacting the ball either too close to your body [5-4] or off to the side, rather than out in front.

D. You may be simply jabbing at the ball with an isolated arm movement, failing to get your body involved in the swing.

CURES:

A. Think *forward* as the serve is hit so you can get into position to make solid contact and return the ball aggressively as often as possible. Concentrate on getting a fast first step on a diagonal toward the net [5-5] and going out to meet the serve. As on your regular groundstrokes, always try to be moving into the shot at impact so your weight comes forward through the ball. A good tactic here (used effectively by Bjorn Borg) is to position yourself well behind the baseline and then start moving forward as your opponent makes his toss. This automatically gets your body in motion and keeps you from thinking defensively.

B. On the forehand backswing, keep your hitting elbow high and away from your body to prevent a

[5-4]

wrist layback problem (as described on page 15). This allows the racket strings to stay in line with the ball right into impact and directs all the energy toward your intended target.

Another good preventive technique is to keep both elbows out in front of your body when in the ready position (as I demonstrated on page 84).

C. On backhands especially, strive to contact the ball comfortably out in front of your body — ideally with your front shoulder out over your front foot at impact [5-6].

D. Against fast and slow serves alike, ingrain into yourself the importance of getting to the ball quickly and turning your body back early whenever possible. By rotating the upper body and stepping forward into the shot, you avoid hitting with an isolated arm movement and allow the body to uncoil into the shot for greater power and consistency. In fact, the slower the serve, the greater your body rotation should be, as you gain more time to step into the ball and take a full topspin stroke off either side.

[5-6]

THE PROBLEM

"I always seem to hit the ball into the net when my opponent attacks behind his serve."

Against a fast serve, when you're swinging with a more compact stroke and your opponent is rushing the net, hitting down on the ball is a "sucker" play — the number-one error on the service return against serve-and-volley players. Instead of forcing your opponent to at least make a play and perhaps mishit his easy volley, you simply net the return and do him the favor.

REASONS:

A. You may be so afraid of giving your opponent a put-away volley that you're forgetting to stroke the return properly.

B. You may be watching your opponent's movements out of the corner of your eye and looking up too early, eager to see where your return is traveling. This early lifting action pulls the front shoulder around and causes the racket to come across on a horizontal path. As we saw in the Forehand and Backhand chapters, this level swing — coupled with the strong pull of gravity on any ball hit relatively flat — generally sends your shot into the net.

C. Your stroke may be fine, but your racket face could be tilted down at impact, sending the ball either short or into the net.

CURES:

A. Reevaluate the psychology at work here between you and the server. Granted, you may feel a bit intimidated by that looming figure coming to the net, but just because your opponent is rushing forward, it doesn't mean that he's totally fearless and invulnerable. In fact, unless he's a talented volleyer, the typical player is praying that you will make an error; he knows that a reasonably decent return will put the pressure on *him* to execute. So the threat of your return can become an effective psychological weapon if he intends to keep coming to the net as part of his normal strategy.

[5-7]

▶ Stroke the ball! Remember, execution is the name of the game. The ball doesn't know the score, doesn't see your opponent coming to the net, and doesn't understand the predicament you're in. All it knows is that if you strike it a certain way it will travel a certain way, so concentrate on the desired stroking pattern and nothing else.

B. Concentrate on keeping your head down through impact [5-7], confident that you will have plenty of time to react to your opponent's next shot.

▶ Instead of letting your eyes roam, zero in on the ball, since it is traveling fast and can easily be misjudged. This also helps keep you from being distracted or flustered by what your opponent is doing on the other side of the net.

C. When you try to land the ball at your opponent's feet — the best antidote against a net-rusher — hit through the shot and finish with a high follow-through to help ensure a return that safely clears

the net. Striving for this high finish will help guarantee a smooth stroke through the hitting zone and should keep you from chopping down at the ball. A high follow-through also counters the racket's natural tendency to drop when the body slows or stops to hit.

Being able to "chip" the ball back at your opponent's feet is an enviable skill, since it forces him to bend low for a half-volley as he moves forward and tries to maintain the offensive. Most players hate to have to scoop for a ball like this because they haven't worked on the half-volley, but hitting your return there with underspin requires an ability that only comes through practice sessions in which you aim for targets near the service line as a partner (or a ball machine) serves the ball.

▶ Think to yourself, "Firm grip, firm wrist, firm forearm," so you contact the ball squarely and negate any rolling action of the racket in the hitting zone, which can send the ball into the net.

THE PROBLEM

"I hit a lot of soft second serves into the net."

REASONS:

A. As you move in to put away your opponent's patty-cake serve, you may be swinging too hard on a level plane, forgetting that you must lift the ball over that high net.

B. You may have a forearm roll-over in the hitting zone, causing the racket face to be closed, or turned down, at impact.

CURES:

A. When your opponent's serve comes in like a helium balloon, play it aggressively but don't get careless. If you're driving the ball with topspin, remember that you're closer to the net than you normally are during a typical baseline rally, and must have a greater vertical lift with the racket to get the ball up and over the net with power and depth. Visualize your target window above the net to help guarantee a good, deep return.

Ideally, of course, you should treat this kind of serve as a typical short-ball opportunity by moving in and hitting the ball deep, as you would an approach shot. When you attack behind your return like this you reduce your opponent's response time and force him to thread the needle with a passing shot.

B. Instead of "playing" with the racket face, concentrate on swinging from the shoulder joint and keeping the wrist fixed to avoid a forearm roll. I find that people with a roll-over problem tend to be timing their roll-overs for fast serves; when the ball comes slowly, their racket heads usually roll early, and the ball goes into the net.

The best cure when you're having trouble driving the ball off a soft second serve is to work on execution rather than on power. As a drill, have a friend hit you a succession of soft serves while you concentrate on hitting regular groundstrokes — safely over the net — and avoid the temptation to slug the ball. Practice these returns over and over again as you determine the speed and the upward angle at which you should be contacting the ball in order to hit your intended on-court targets.

THE PROBLEM

"I always feel defensive on the backhand side."

I've found over the years that many players have pretty good confidence in their forehand return, but think, "Do I have time for a quick prayer?" when they see strong serves coming to their backhand side. This isn't surprising, for the backhand side is far less forgiving to the person who wants to return the ball aggressively but succumbs to several fatal flaws. (Two-handed hitters tend to have greater confidence because they are swinging with certain forehand characteristics.)

REASONS:

You may not be respecting the fact that you must respond faster against serves to the backhand in order to contact the ball out in front of your body. There's almost always enough time to take a sufficient swing on the forehand side, since the shoulder housing the racket arm is away from the net, and physiologically it's not hard to salvage a late "arm" swing when you have no other choice. But these advantages don't apply to the backhand, where lateness in reaching the serve is much more destructive. You may manage to get the ball back over the net, but without any real pace or accuracy. And that's not good enough against an opponent who knows how to move in against these weak returns. In fact, when you fail to get into position early enough, you're forced to swing all arm, which means relying on your extensor muscles for power. Those muscles can't handle this stress on one backhand after another against a strong server.

If you're always arriving late on the backhand side and forgetting that the shoulder housing the hitting arm is on the front side of your body, you are being forced into a defensive style of play. You may want to play offensively, but all you can do is either block the return or try to hit with underspin.

CURES:

Learn to respond faster against serves to the backhand side so you can rotate your upper body, step toward the net, and uncoil into the shot as often as possible. This means, for one thing, that you must avoid playing with the same rhythm on the backhand as on the forehand. Quicken your movements and try to reach the serve with enough time to be able to contact the ball out in front of your body, so you can improve your chances of driving the return with topspin or floating it deep with underspin. Even though a hard serve may not allow you time enough to take a full backhand stroke, you can still turn your upper body and gain the uncoiling action that will transfer into the shot and help you utilize the server's speed. (Meeting the ball early is not so crucial if you are going to chip the ball back with underspin, since in that case you are contacting it almost even with the hitting shoulder.)

If you tend to be slightly late against players who serve fast, be careful not to fall into the trap of also being slightly late against those who serve slowly. This can easily happen if you start loafing a bit and pacing yourself rhythmically with the speed your opponent has on the ball, rather than simply concentrating on reaching every ball as quickly as possible.

THE PROBLEM

"My opponent is killing me with his slice serve."

[5-8]
[5-9]

Actually, you'll rarely play an opponent who can consistently slice a serve from the deuce court and drive you into the side fence. A player with that kind of serving ability is usually on the pro tour. However, if a particular opponent is acing you with a slice serve on key points, then he's capitalizing on your positioning and coverage weaknesses.

REASONS:

A. You may be overplaying the backhand side by standing too far to the left in your ready position, which opens you up to a serve sliced wide to your forehand.

B. You may not be anticipating the slice serve and getting a fast first step toward the ball.

C. You may be running wide for the ball—too nearly parallel to the baseline—which forces you to run longer and places you on the defensive if your opponent comes to the net.

D. When you chase a slice serve toward the right fence, you may be succumbing to a common temptation: hitting your return down the line, to a right-hander's backhand. Unfortunately, this forces you to hit down a narrow lane, into a tiny target area, and your opponent can now pull across and hit a crummy backhand that forces you to hit your own backhand—on the run.

CURES:

A. Instead of trying (consciously or unconsciously) to protect a weak backhand by standing too far to the left in your ready position, play *halfway* between the extremes of your opponent's potential serving range on either side. Then go to work on your backhand.

B. Anticipate the slice serve by learning to read your opponent's toss and hitting motion. Most opponents, except those at the pro level, tip off their intentions of hitting a big slice by tossing the ball way off to the side [5-8] compared to their normal toss [5-9].

C. After your eyes give you an early tip-off, your feet must respond. Work hard to get a fast first step

toward the ball, and try to move in on a *diagonal* in order to cut off the serve's angle before it gets wide and forces you into a defensive return. Moving forward on the diagonal will give you a chance to return the ball more aggressively.

D. When running wide, return most balls crosscourt, thus tempting your opponent with a risky down-the-line shot to your backhand. Hit the ball relatively high and deep if he stays back after serving, since you simply want to gain time to move into a good position for your next shot.

CHAPTER 6

The Approach Shot

THE PROBLEM

"When I come to the net behind my approach shot, I usually get passed."

Eventually, the approach shot should become one of your bread-and-butter weapons, since it allows you to play an attacking game from the baseline and sets up effective net play. Unfortunately, this shot could also be putting you, rather than your opponent, in deep trouble.

REASONS:

A. You may be moving in against balls outside your short-ball range. As a result, you're not advancing far enough to cut down your opponent's passing angles and reach advantageous volleying positions that would give you control of the rally.

B. Your approach shot may be landing too short and may be placed in the wrong spot, giving your opponent too much time and too good a hitting angle.

Remember my adage: "People who attack behind a short approach shot tend to lose at a faster rate." Not only are you allowing your opponent to step inside the baseline and tee off, you're also shortening the time you have to reach an ideal volleying position in order to cut off his passing shot.

C. You may be stopping to hit your approach shot. This not only causes accuracy problems (see page 98), but also keeps you from gaining a positional advantage for your next shot by stranding you in "no-man's-land," that area near the service line where balls seem harder to hit and you get that sitting-duck feeling against a hard hitter.

D. You may be neglecting the approach shot in practice. I've found over the years that this is the most neglected important shot in the game, at every level of play.

[6-1]

CURES:

A. Make sure that you are advancing only against balls that are going to land in your short-ball range (unless you're trying to surprise your opponent by moving in for a midcourt volley the moment he drops his head to hit a groundstroke). This range (shown in 6-1) is the area on court from which you can hit an approach shot while on the move and then be able to reach a point midway between the net and the service line just as, or before, your opponent hits the ball.

B. Learn to hit your approach shot crisp and deep to minimize your opponent's offensive opportunities. If you can consistently land the ball inside a five-foot-square box at either baseline corner or right down the middle [6-2], you'll keep your opponent off bal-

ance and hitting from a defensive position, and at the same time you'll increase your available reaction time as the volleyer if he tries to drive the ball. By hitting with depth you gain more time to get close to the net, which creates much narrower passing-shot lanes for your opponent and widens your potential volleying angles.

C. Since your goal is to advance as close to the net as possible, move in quickly and "run through" your shot [6-3 through 6-5, overleaf] so you reach a *temporary* ready position [6-6] equidistant from the potential passing shots your opponent can hit either down the line or cross-court. From here you want to either move forward to volley or turn and run back for a lob.

(continued)

[6-2]

[6-3]

[6-4]

[6-5]

When hitting the approach shot on the move, turn slightly sideways to the net and contact the ball off your front shoulder so body energy can supply most of your power while momentum carries you forward.

D. Take time to work on the approach shot in practice, with a partner or against a ball machine. One thing you need to discover is whether you should hit this shot flat (where you're swinging on a horizontal plane), with underspin, or with topspin — whichever proves most comfortable and accurate with your stroking style. Then drill, running in for the short ball that lands around your service line and aiming for target areas in both corners and down the middle. Try setting up tennis cans inside these target areas, for they provide positive feedback when they are sent flying. Practicing like this will also help you realize (1) how high over the net you must hit the ball in order to have it land deep and (2) how you must adjust to different hitting angles as you contact the ball on the rise, at the peak of its bounce, or on the downflight.

If you don't have time to practice, work on the approach shot in matches against opponents who hit lots of patty-cake serves and short balls from the baseline.

THE PROBLEM

"I hit too many approach shots into the net."

REASONS:

A. You may be stopping to hit the ball, and the laws of physics are killing your shot. Think about your tennis swing and your approach shot in relation to a moving automobile. When you abruptly apply the brakes, the front end of a car goes down and the back end goes up. Similarly, if you're moving toward the net and stop to hit your approach shot, the upper body and the arm keep going forward and down. And what happens to the racket? Unless you compensate, it goes down along with the arm, and the ball either catches the net or falls short on your opponent's side of the court. Also, by delaying your forward momentum you keep yourself from crowding the net for a follow-up volley.

B. You may be arriving late and contacting the ball on the downflight at too low a position in relation to the net. When the ball is dropping like this and is below net-tape level, you face an obvious problem if you're trying to hit straight through the ball or intending to impart underspin.

C. Depending on your stroking style:

▶ The racket face may be facing downward at impact, either out of carelessness or because you are rolling the racket face over in the hitting zone with unwanted forearm action.

▶ If you're swinging level, you may be aiming too close to the net, forgetting about gravity's downward pull on the ball and the fact that the net remains a high barrier even as you move in from the baseline.

▶ If you're hitting with underspin (most likely on the backhand side), you may be hitting down at too sharp an angle and finishing with the racket at around knee level [6-7].

CURES:

A. Run through the shot as you stroke the ball [6-8], and keep moving forward. This will help keep your racket traveling up and out toward your intended target area and will allow you to gain a good volleying position near the net [6-9].

[6-7]

B. Work on your anticipation and on taking a fast first step toward an opponent's short ball so you can contact the ball at the peak of its bounce as often as possible. Keeping in mind your short-ball range as your opponent goes to hit a groundstroke, remind yourself that the ball should land short; statistics show that people hit short much more often than deep. Be surprised when you see the ball coming deep, not when you see that it's going to land short. Then learn to trust your instincts, breaking quickly forward when you sense the opportunity.

C. Always strive to hit through the ball and finish with a high follow-through [6-10]. This high finish helps ensure a desired stroking pattern — up and out, not down — as your racket comes through the hitting zone. Finishing high with the racket also leaves you ready for the volley as you move to the net.

▶ Here's where it's again important to know your target window over the net. When you visualize a target area that is safely above the net rather than on the court and try to hit through the window, the ball tends to stay clear of the net.

THE PROBLEM

"My approach shots are going too long."

REASON:

If this is your problem, you'll almost always find that the racket face is open, or laid back too much, at impact [6-11] instead of being relatively straight up and down [6-12]. One possible cause: you're trying to contact the ball too far out in front of your body, which tilts the racket skyward.

CURE:

In practice sessions, consciously close the racket face in the hitting zone as you aim for target areas above

the net and inside your opponent's baseline. This type of exaggeration is often necessary to break comfortable but incorrect habits as you strike the ball. Then concentrate on keeping the wrist and forearm as a fixed unit coming into the hitting zone to help guarantee a correctly positioned racket face at impact, one shot after another [6-12]. Also, strive to hit the ball firmly, without a floppy racket, and avoid babying the shot just to keep it in play. Have your target area clearly fixed in your head as you move to the ball, so that you're mentally free to hit and you can learn what it means to be offensive with this shot.

[6-11]

[6-12]

THE PROBLEM

"I'm confused about whether to hit flat or with underspin or topspin."

REASON:

You haven't gone out and practiced all three styles to find out which one you can control best as you move toward the net, and which one suits your particular approach to the game.

CURES:

Practice hitting approach shots flat, with underspin, and with topspin against a ball machine, with a coach, or with a friend. Set up target areas on the court but aim the ball through your target window over the net. Then when you go into a match you'll know which particular style is best suited to your ability and temperament off either side, because you'll have tested it out.

On the forehand side, I'd recommend hitting either flat or with topspin so you can drive the ball hard and deep. This will pay off when your opponent is out of position and you want to nail the ball and

decrease his available reaction and recovery time. Of course, the harder you hit your approach shot, the less time you have to get into position for a subsequent volley. If you want to hit the approach shot flat, you can swing almost straight across, provided that you contact the ball when it is higher than net level, and finish with a high follow-through.

On the backhand side, most experienced players tend to chip (underspin) their backhand approaches. They know that when they underspin this shot deep, as opposed to hitting hard with topspin, the ball floats through the air longer and helps them buy time to gain a better volleying position. A ball hit with underspin also travels on a lower arc than one hit with topspin, meaning that it will bounce lower as it comes off the court, forcing an opponent to bend down and hit up. Ideally, this will give you an easier put-away volley at the net.

Still, you must *practice* hitting your approach shot with underspin because it's a difficult shot to control under pressure.

THE PROBLEM

"I have a lot of trouble controlling my underspin backhand approach shots."

REASONS:

A. Like many players, you may be swinging like a lumberjack, slicing down at the ball with too severe a high-to-low motion, which is sending many of your shots into the net. The steeper or more severe your high-to-low angle into the ball, the more open the racket face must be and the more calculations you must make to position it perfectly in relation to the incoming ball.

B. You may be adding a destructive bit of racket-head play in the hitting zone, thinking you must curl or slice under the ball to give your shot the desired underspin effect.

CURES:

A. Learn a high-low-high stroking pattern that resembles an inverted bow (as illustrated in 3-36 through 3-38) so the racket face is not traveling down at such a severe angle as it comes through the hitting zone. You must still strike the ball on the downflight to produce underspin, but now you can do so with greater safety. A high finish encourages and reinforces this desired overall stroking pattern.

B. Since the ball is on the racket strings for only an instant—actually about four milliseconds—concentrate on keeping the wrist and forearm as a fixed unit coming into the hitting zone, with the racket only slightly beveled back at impact. Now practice what it means to let the high-low-high motion of your swing, as opposed to fancy racket play, impart underspin. You can use extra racket bevel to increase the underspin, but this requires perfect timing. You should focus instead on the racket's downward path into the shot and your overall stroking motion.

Once again, you must practice hitting your approach shot with underspin because it's difficult to control this shot under pressure.

CHAPTER 7

The Volley

THE PROBLEM

"I'm continually hitting the ball into the net."

REASONS:

When your volleys are continually finding the net and driving you crazy—as we saw happen to Ivan Lendl in the 1987 Wimbledon finals against Pat Cash —either you're swinging down at the ball or the racket face is slightly turned down in the hitting zone. So let's pay attention to these usual suspects:

A. You may be forgetting just how high the net is, even when you volley from a point halfway between it and the service line [7-1]. The photograph shows that a six-footer must actually look *through* the net to see his opponent's service box—a typical target area for those short-angle volleys we all love to try to hit when we're about 10 or 12 feet from the net. Obviously it doesn't pay to hit down against most volleys if you want the ball to clear the net safely.

B. You may be stopping as you volley, which brings the racket face down—as well as the ball. Think about my analogy to a car when the brakes are applied: the front end goes down and the rear end comes up (see page 98).

C. You may be letting the wrist go soft or floppy as you stretch forward or extend out to the side to volley.

D. As the ball approaches, you may be facing the net, intending to "push" the ball safely (though weakly) over the net. But when you are facing forward, the racket invariably comes up near your ear and bevels back, making timing critical. If you are slightly early at impact—contacting the ball too far out in front—the racket face will be tilted down [7-2], and the ball will usually go into the net.

E. You may be too careless with what appear to be easy, put-away volleys.

[7-2] [7-3]

[7-1]

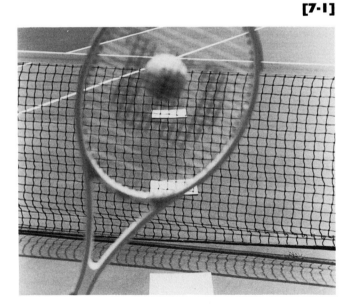

CURES:

A. Since the slightest down-hit will kill you on most volleys (unless you compensate by having the racket face tilted back), aim for a target window safely above the net. Instead of thinking about a specific target area on the court, concentrate on punching the ball through this window; this will reinforce the importance of hitting out—as if swinging across a high tabletop—and not down. When practicing, have a friend hold a racket up at the net, and aim for different heights on the racket from different volleying positions on the court. Here [7-3], I'm aiming for a cardboard X strung above the net in order to hit my on-court target. Also notice how high the net is when I volley from the service line.

B. Keep moving as you go to volley so you help ensure a solid hit while setting yourself up for a more advantageous follow-up volley, if it should prove to be necessary. The exception here is when you have no choice but to simply stretch wide for a well-angled passing shot.

C. When stretching to volley, and when forced to contact the ball at a point below net level, keep your hitting arm up as best you can, and the racket face beveled slightly back. Try to maintain a firm wrist and forearm position so your racket head can stay above wrist level whenever possible.

D. Turn sideways to the net as you go to volley so you'll be free to punch through the ball with a crisp, compact stroking motion out toward your intended target. Try to contact the ball at around eye level, just about even with your front shoulder. Ideally, use your knees as elevators to lower and raise your body so that, as often as possible, your racket, your eyes, and the ball are all at the same level at impact. This helps ensure the best hitting angle and encourages you to bend low for those tough volleys below net level [7-4], which you must lift up with a slightly open racket face.

E. Move quickly to *all* volley opportunities so you are hitting above net level as often as possible. Otherwise, when an opponent hits a weak drive from the baseline, your natural tendency will be to relax and forget about moving forward to cut off the ball as early as you can; then suddenly the ball will lose speed and drop below net level, forcing a defensive volley that can easily catch the net cord—especially if you let the wrist and racket go limp.

THE PROBLEM

"I often hit easy drop volleys into the net."

Every so often, when you go to the net to volley and somebody hits you a little dinky shot, do you think, "I'll just hold my racket here and drop the ball over the net"? And then does the ball come off and hit you in the foot? And do you think, "Jeez, I was almost cheating—how could I have missed that shot so close to the net"?

REASON:

You've forgotten about basic laws of physics related to incident and reflected angles. If you're holding your racket perfectly fixed and vertical, a high volley will leave your strings at the same angle at which it arrived, meaning that it usually travels down your thigh or into the net [7-5]. Gravity is also pulling the ball lower as it nears you, exaggerating the problem when you hold the racket still.

CURE:

Even against a "gimme" shot from your opponent, you must have some forward movement and a firm

[7-5]

racket position as you go to strike the ball. This forward movement counteracts the ball's angle coming in and helps send it safely over the net [7-6]. Also, maintain a firm grip through impact, even when you try to finesse a drop-shot winner. When most players try to soften their grip, they do so too early.

[7-6]

THE PROBLEM

"When I try to volley a cross-court passing shot down the line, the ball often goes out of bounds."

REASON:

This is a shot we all tend to miss when we forget about the laws of physics and try to follow the common advice, "Pick out your target on the volley and aim for that target." Unfortunately, the ball doesn't always travel straight for the target when you're volleying a sharp-angled passing shot. Unless you compensate, it will go off the racket strings at the same angle at which it arrives.

For example, let's say you're coming to the net and your opponent hits a cross-court passing shot to your forehand. You want to punch a volley down the line, into his backhand corner, but you fail to counteract the ball's angle as it arrives. As a result, when

the racket comes through, aimed at the backhand corner, the ball rebounds off the strings and travels out of bounds, as indicated by the line of cards in the photograph [7-7].

CURE:

When going for down-the-line winners against cross-court drives, take physics into account by aiming your volley for a point between the spot where the ball was struck by your opponent and your desired target, where you want the ball to actually land. In the photograph, this means aiming for the X in order to hit the O when you are hitting the ball hard.

[7-7]

THE PROBLEM

"Many of my volleys go too long."

REASONS:

If this is your problem, you'll almost always find that your racket face is turned under or laid back at impact, which sends the ball high and long. Occasionally your target window over the net may be too high or you may be hitting too hard, but these mistakes seldom cause trouble at the club level. Instead, the problem usually stems from one or both of these two culprits:

A. You may be facing the net as you swing [7-8], which means that the racket face has only a brief moment to contact the ball properly; if you are slightly late at impact, the strings will be laid back instead of vertical.

B. Your hitting elbow may be incorrectly positioned on the backswing, either tucked in near the body on the forehand (as I'm demonstrating in 7-8) or raised high on the backhand [7-10]. In both instances this elbow action lays the racket head back.

CURES:

A. Make sure that your body is turned sideways and your shoulders are relatively perpendicular to the net as you strike the ball [7-9 and 7-11]. Also notice in both photographs that my hitting arm is extended out and away from my body.

B. Check your hitting elbow on both sides.

▶ If the elbow is too close to your body on the forehand backswing, push it up as you rotate the upper body to take the racket back. This will keep the racket face from tilting back as the elbow leads the way on the backswing and will help guarantee a vertical racket face at impact, on a path with the incoming ball.

▶ On the backhand, instead of having the hitting elbow raised and bent on the backswing, strive to keep it low, while maintaining an extended arm all the way through impact, as shown in 7-11.

THE PROBLEM

"I never really know <u>where</u> my volley is going to land."

REASONS:

A. My bet is that you're trying to do too much with the racket as you swing.

▶ You may be coming in with the racket head purposely laid back [7-12] so you can snap your wrist into the shot. This wristiness can help generate a bit more power, but it requires you to judge — under pressure — how and when to snap your wrist for an accurate shot. A few top players can lay the racket back like this because they have the experience and the ability to time the shot properly. Everyone else tends to lack this touch, resulting in an inconsistent, unpredictable racket-face position at impact.

▶ Your swing may simply be too long and, as a result, too unwieldly in the hitting zone as you strive for greater power. Remember, the greater the length of your swing — on groundstrokes and volleys alike — the greater your talent must be.

B. You may be playing a "one-grip game" by holding a Continental, which undermines consistency while demanding greater skill and a stronger wrist and forearm than an Eastern grip. Whether the volley is low or high, the Continental keeps you from thinking "palm to my target" on the forehand and "knuckles to my target" on the backhand as you stroke the ball. Instead, you must place greater faith in touch and timing.

[7-12]

[7-13]

hand) or knuckles (on the backhand) reach out as if to intercept the ball. Think about simply turning your shoulders to get your racket into position and then stepping forward to meet the ball.

B. Reconsider the Continental grip and learn to hold an Eastern grip on both sides, just as I advocated for baseline groundstrokes (pages 16 and 37). You'll hear the argument that there's insufficient time to switch grips when you must volley on one side and then on the other, but our research shows that players can switch grips faster than they can take a single step, since the hands move faster than the feet. Learning to switch grips quickly is a skill that requires some practice in order for it to become second nature.

[7-14]

CURES:

A. Two key concepts are involved as you work to curb excessive racket-head play.

▶ First, learn to volley while maintaining the wrist, the racket, and the hitting arm as a fixed unit. This will keep your racket strings directly in line with the incoming ball [7-13] and will help ensure a vertical racket face at impact. By preventing the racket from rolling over or turning under in the hitting zone you gain much more latitude for making solid contact on one volley after another.

▶ Second, instead of thinking that you must take a long backswing in order to volley the ball hard, strive for a firm, punching motion that utilizes upper body rotation—and the speed of your opponent's shot—for power. On both sides, rotate your front shoulder away from the ball as you move toward the shot [7-14], then have your hitting palm (on the fore-

THE PROBLEM

"I can't seem to hit many winning volleys."

Are you good at keeping the ball in play with your volleys but weak at converting those volleys into outright winners? If so, then no doubt you're frustrated by your inability to hit a put-away volley when the opportunity arises; instead you simply allow your opponent to keep playing the point, and very likely he suddenly wins it himself. That's enough to send you to chess, I know, but first let's look at the important physical *and* mental factors that are keeping you from winning points with your volley.

REASONS:

A. Your volleying technique may be keeping you from hitting the ball hard and accurately.

B. Whatever your technique, you may be undermining the potential of your volley by being unnecessarily late, with the result that you either don't reach your hitting position early enough or have to volley too far from the net. Here are some examples of how you may be getting into trouble:

[7-15]

[7-16]

▶ When you're near the net, you may be settling into a flat-footed ready position [7-15] as you watch your opponent hit from the baseline. This leaves you poorly prepared to move quickly toward a volley opportunity.

▶ You may be fearful and indecisive at the net, afraid to trust your instincts as you watch your opponent strike the ball. This slows your movement to the ball and leaves you in a defensive hitting position against a good passing shot.

▶ You may be backing away from the net and letting the ball come to you, or you may be moving parallel to the net as you go to volley. As a result, the ball often drops below net level, and you turn an offensive opening into a lunging defensive effort.

▶ You may be stopping as you volley. Not only does this lessen your ability to hit the ball aggressively, it can keep you from crowding the net for a follow-up volley.

CURES:

A. Work on the stroking technique suggestions in this chapter, then increase your power potential by learning to transfer your body weight from the back to the front foot just before ball contact. By turning your upper body on the backswing and having a forward body movement at impact, you can begin to hit hard, accurate volleys that either force weak returns or are outright winners. Make sure that you are turning your shoulders to initiate the backswing so you can uncoil your upper body into the shot. A short, compact swing is important for control, but a body coil can add impressive power to that control and give your volleys a distinctive "pop" as you close off the point.

B. I tell my students, "The closer you are to the net, the less talent you need to be a good volleyer. The converse is also true: the farther back you are, the more talent you must have." With those adages in mind, here are some tips that can help you become a better offensive volleyer:

► When you reach a momentary ready position as your opponent goes to hit from the baseline, be ready to break in any direction [7-16]. If you let your feet fall asleep, they can't get you to the ball in time to make you famous. You may not be swift of foot, but if you can get a quick first step toward your opponent's passing shot — ideally on a forward diagonal — you'll greatly improve your volleying angles.

► Whenever possible, run through your first volley as you approach the net and keep closing in so you can maximize your volleying angles while at the same time reducing your opponent's potential passing angles. If I volley the ball (or hit an approach shot) down the middle and deep and reach an ideal ready position [7-17], my opponent has only 61 feet for his cross-court passing attempt — and few living players can hit that kind of severe topspin to pass an opponent at the net. Also notice in the photograph that I'm ready to break in either direction.

(continued)

[7-17]

▶ Think aggressively and trust your instincts as you play the net. Instead of trying to confirm every decision—"Is he going to pass me on the left or on the right? . . . Son-of-a-gun, it was to my backhand" —break one way or the other the instant your opponent hits the ball, if not sooner. You may run the wrong way at times, but that's how you're going to improve, by forcing yourself to go with your initial decision. With experience you'll find that your "guesses" become quite educated.

▶ When practicing, avoid simply volleying the ball toward your partner at the baseline. Aim for the corners, reinforcing the idea that most volleys should end the point—not simply keep the ball in play.

▶ Don't forget: the closer you can get to the net, the more you'll bolster your put-away potential by giving yourself a higher ball to volley and opening up wider volleying angles. For example, contrast my potential effectiveness as a volleyer in the two photo-

[7-19]

graphs [7-18 and 7-19]. In the first instance, I'm volleying ten feet from the net, and I have only a 30-degree hitting angle over the net to my opponent's court. Few players can hit a winning cross-court, short-angled volley from this position. But notice how much I open up the court and my hitting angles when I can get two steps closer to the net. Wouldn't you rather be volleying from this position as often as possible? Not only do you have a much greater safety margin over the net as you go for a short-angled winner, you also reduce the time your opponent has in which to reach the ball.

Seen from another perspective [7-20], when I can get two steps forward from my momentary ready position as I see my opponent go to drive the ball, I can easily cut off his very best cross-court passing attempt (which is 65 feet 9 inches on the diagonal) by taking just one step to my left. I have a much greater distance to cover when I camp at the X and move laterally.

THE PROBLEM

"I can't control my half-volley."

Are you one of those players who runs halfway to the net, gets a ball at the feet, and says, "Take two, I don't play anything hit below the knees"? Are you tempted to kick at a ball coming off the court like this because you can't do much better with a racket? If so, lacking a reliable half-volley, you are undermining your ability to play an aggressive serve-and-volley type of game.

REASONS:

A. You may be coming in and trying to scoop the ball over the net with the racket face tilted slightly up. Doing this against a hard-hit ball that is rising off the court at a sharp angle (for example a service return) usually sends the ball quite high.

B. You may be trying to simply "arm" the ball over the net, instead of using the strength in your thighs. The result is usually a wobbly, inconsistent racket face at impact.

CURES:

A. Take advantage of the ball's incoming angle off the court by having the racket face vertical or slightly tilted down as you contact the ball on the rise. Notice in the photographs [7-21 and 7-22] that my racket is facing slightly down before and at impact and then moves forward and up after the hit [7-23].

B. Get low to the ball by using your thigh muscles and knee bend and maintain a firm hitting arm so the racket head is solid as you come through the shot with a rising motion. This will help the ball to clear the net safely and travel deep. A high finish with the hitting arm and body also helps you continue moving forward, ready to volley an opponent's passing shot.

▶ Position your body sideways to the net as you go to hit the ball [7-21], keep your head down through impact, and maintain your forward momentum in

[7-21]

[7-22]

order not to lose valuable steps to the net position. As you hit the ball, just keep right on going to the net behind your aggressive new half-volley. Now you can have some fun getting balls hit at your feet, since you're no longer simply playing with the racket and dumping the ball into the net or laying it over the back fence.

Basically, the half-volley is a reflex shot that allows you little time to think about execution; you're charging the net, the ball is coming low and hard, and you rarely get a good look at it (though you should strive to keep your eyes on the ball, as timing is crucial). Therefore, the only real way to master the correct instincts is to practice this shot off a ball machine or against a friend who can stand on the other side of the net and hit balls at your feet. This will help you determine (1) the best angle at which to hold your racket in the hitting zone, (2) how much you have to bend, and (3) how it feels kinesthetically to execute the shot accurately.

[7-23]

THE PROBLEM

"I keep getting burned by the lob when I come to the net."

Do you tend to camp at the net in your ready position, watching your opponent and thinking, "Uh-oh—he's going to lob"? And then, instead of matching these instincts with quick reactions, do you simply stand there, look back over your shoulder, and mutter, "Nuts, he did it again"? If so, it's not surprising that you often get beaten by an ordinary, put-away type of lob.

REASON:

You may not be trusting your instincts, or respecting the fact that a fast retreat can neutralize the best of lobs.

CURE:

When you're at the net, poised in your ready position, study your opponent's racket-head movement as he swings—and don't be afraid to react. If he's sitting back on his back foot and his racket face has dropped low and is tilted back [7-24], there's no way he's going to drive the ball. So quickly turn and retreat for a lob. Take three quick steps back, and you'll find that you have time to reach virtually any lob. Now you might be thinking, "Yeah, Vic, but what if I turn and run back and my opponent goes, 'Aha! I tricked you!' and then drives the ball?" Well, rest assured that in all likelihood you won't be playing people who have the ability to switch successfully from a lob to a passing shot like this.

[7-24]

CHAPTER 8

The Overhead

THE PROBLEM

"I'm usually late when I retreat for an overhead."

REASON:

You could be letting your feet fall asleep as you watch your opponent move to the ball along the baseline — and you may be afraid to trust your instincts.

Many players are able to make fantastic decisions in their net position — "The guy's going to lob!" — but then wait to confirm their judgment before they move. This hesitation at the net keeps them from capitalizing on overhead opportunities, especially in club tennis, where few players can consistently make their lobs land deep.

CURE:

When you're near the net, you should be thinking, "Drive or lob, drive or lob?" as you study your opponent's stroking motion and the position of his racket face as it nears impact. Then, in order to hit an overhead smash against nearly any lob, just turn and retreat quickly the moment you see the lob coming [8-1]. Take three or four long steps, then use short, quick steps to position yourself for the hit. Try to move back deeper than the ball so you have time to move forward and make contact ahead of your body.

[8-1]

120

THE PROBLEM

"I'm hitting my overheads too long."

REASONS:

A. Lateness may be killing you. You may not be respecting the fact that an opponent's lob, unlike your service toss, is closing in at a speed that can easily catch you unprepared. As a result, you may be moving too slowly to your anticipated hitting position or starting your swing too late, which keeps you from hitting up and out, just as you do on the serve.

B. If you feel that you are swinging correctly, then you may well be letting the ball get behind you as you go to hit. This causes the racket face to be laid back at impact, sending the ball long.

CURES:

A. Move quickly into a good hitting position and start your body rotation and backswing earlier than you do now so you can hit up through the ball.

Use virtually the same stroking motion that I advocate on the serve, with one exception: shorten the backswing by simply taking the racket back at eye level, then turn forward and let the racket loop behind your back as you go to swing up at the ball.

B. Strive to make contact farther out in front of your hitting shoulder, until you start hitting the ball into play. Ideally, in fact, you should be contacting the ball out in front and slightly off to your right — the same contact position as on the serve. What you want to avoid when you keep hitting beyond the baseline is the temptation to try to adjust by hitting down on the ball.

An equally destructive concept, and a common trap, is to think that you should start easing off and aiming for your opponent's midcourt area. This simply gives him a reprieve and the incentive to keep lobbing when he's in trouble, knowing that he can't really get hurt by one of your overheads.

THE PROBLEM

"I keep smashing the ball into the net."

REASONS:

A. You may have been led to believe that you must hit down against a dropping ball in order to bring it down into your opponent's court. This works well only when you're right in front of the net as you hit.

B. Your chin may be dropping just before impact, which means that your upper body is pulling down—as well as the racket face [8-2]. The ball usually follows, right into the net.

C. You may be too casual about your preparation for the overhead, and as a result the ball is dropping too low in front of your body as you swing.

CURES:

A. Concentrate on swinging UP at this falling ball—not down—in order for it to go forward, safely over the net toward your intended target area. A research effort with physicist Dr. Patrick Keating has shown that when a ball is dropping at a 45-degree angle off a lob, the racket face must be vertical at impact and traveling upward at about an eight-degree angle just to counteract the severe angle of the incoming ball. You must contact the ball with an upward force to overcome its drop and send it deep.

▶ When hitting overheads from behind the service line, concentrate on depth and ignore the temptation

[8-2]

to go for a short-angled winner, since few players can do this consistently from the backcourt without catching the net or going wide. Even when your opponent is already behind the baseline and bracing for your overhead smash, he'll rarely give you trouble if you simply hit the ball hard and deep to either corner or, as a surprise, right down the middle.

▶ Since the natural tendency, especially on key points, is to pull down and hit the ball short or into the net, try to establish a pattern of hitting long early in the match and then gradually shortening your shot if necessary. Do this by contacting the ball farther out in front of your body—but still swinging up. You may hit several balls beyond the baseline at first, but you'll be lethal as you find your overhead range. When you get into pressure situations you'll have the confidence to hit hard and deep because you've been treating the overhead as an offensive weapon and you're comfortable hitting hard with your normal swing. In contrast, most people start out a match hitting short—and never adjust. Then,

when the pressure's on, they're afraid to hit the hard, deep shot that's needed because they haven't tested that area near the baseline. Instead they simply ease off just to make sure that they get the ball in play on this big point.

B. Make sure that you keep your chin up through impact [8-3] to keep the upper body from sagging. A good trick is to count one beat after striking the ball before allowing yourself to look down. This insures against your pulling down too early. You'll have plenty of time to see where your shot is traveling.

C. Keep your feet moving as you try to get into a comfortable hitting position as early as possible. Remember: you're preparing for a ball that is falling from a greater height and at a faster speed than your service toss (which, ideally, should be contacted at or near its peak). This means that your timing in the hitting zone is critical, for you have only an instant to contact the ball at a desired point. So be aggressive, and don't wait for the ball to come to you.

THE PROBLEM

"I'm afraid to smash the overhead."

Are you reluctant to hit the overhead as hard as you hit the serve? Are you inhibited by the memory of the many times you've choked this shot, knocking the ball into the back fence or down into the net, and would you rather just keep the rally alive by simply poking the ball back to your opponent? Playing it safe may be comforting, but you undermine your game by choosing to baby every overhead opportunity. A smart opponent, for example, will start feeding you nothing but lobs whenever he's in trouble because he knows you won't try to end the point as he scrambles into a better position. Moreover, when you forsake an aggressive overhead, you can't afford to attack the net behind your serve or an approach shot if your opponent can lob.

REASONS:

A. You may not be appreciating the overhead's potential as a home-run type of shot.

B. You may not have worked on the shot in practice enough to gain the necessary confidence.

CURES:

A. Without being reckless, you should try to "deck" the ball hard and deep as often as possible,

especially against short lobs when you're in control of the point. Even if your opponent manages to return the shot, at least you won't have given him an easy reprieve, and he'll know that you'll always threaten to end points with a big bomb. You'll miss an occasional overhead hitting like this, but it's a far better way of playing than merely punching the ball like Mickey Mouse the entire match.

B. While you're learning to regard the overhead as a power play, get out and practice so you can begin to sense that you indeed "own" this shot. This is a "confidence" stroke that demands a great deal of practice, for I've observed that generally there's little middle ground: people have either a good overhead or a crummy one.

One reason most players have trouble with the overhead is that they find it hard to gauge when and where to contact that falling ball—a skill you can only acquire by hitting a ton of overheads. The overhead is one of the most difficult shots in tennis because you see the ball coming in against the sky (or the roof), and there's no background to help your depth perception. Thus it's quite difficult—without a lot of practice—to judge the ball's speed and the angle at which it is falling, and to know when you should start your upward swing and where to make contact.

THE PROBLEM

"I often miss the 'cripple' overhead."

How often does this happen to you on a tennis court? Your opponent is way out of court, you're at the net, and he hits you a little dinky lob — but you proceed to blast the ball out of play or into the net. This blunder probably triggers more frustration than any other missed shot in tennis, and it gives your opponent an enormous lift. In fact, most people tend to miss their next overhead too because they're so angry about the one they just bungled.

Here are some tips that can help you avoid this situation.

REASONS:

A. You may be falling prey to a problem common to many players, pros included: a tendency to underplay and underestimate a slow, short lob. Even the easiest put-away lob demands good footwork and positioning by the hitter, yet for some reason people seldom rush to get there and put it away. Instead they often seem to almost assume the personality of the lob itself; it's a slow and slovenly shot, so they take the same approach. They fall into a trap of pacing their movement with the ball — when the ball comes slowly, they almost walk into position. And as a result the ball ends up falling too close to their heads or too low out in front.

B. You may be equally careless with your stroking technique. Very often, for example, players forget to rotate their upper body as they prepare to bomb an innocent-looking lob, and they frequently ignore the importance of hitting up and out at the ball.

CURE:

A and B. Remember that even a sitting-duck type of lob demands respect if you plan to hit your overhead with power and accuracy. So stop loafing as

[8-4]

you move to the ball, and pay careful attention to your stroking technique — for example, upper-body rotation as you swing [8-4]. You may think that a lack of concentration could be a factor in your missed overheads, but be careful that you're not trying to concentrate on the wrong thing. Instead of telling yourself, "Put this easy one away," try focusing on your footwork or on a specific element of technique.

THE PROBLEM

"I have trouble generating power on the overhead."

REASONS:

A. You may be letting the ball drop too low or fall too far behind your body before going up to hit it, thus cramping your swing.

B. You may be pointing your finger too early at the incoming ball in order to track its path **[8-5]**. Unfortunately, this inhibits the upper-body rotation you need to hit a smooth, powerful overhead. See for yourself how hard it is to point to the sky and then rotate your body trunk to set up an uncoiling action when you swing up and out at the ball. You'd have to be triple-jointed to make all your body segments work in sequence.

CURES:

A. Reach your intended hitting position as early as possible so that you're free to start your swing early and can stretch up to meet the ball comfortably out in front of your hitting shoulder and above your head.

[8-6]

[8-7]

B. Instead of being an early "finger pointer," turn or coil your upper body as you prepare to swing [8-6], then track the incoming ball with a bent left elbow until you rotate into the shot [8-7]. Now let the left arm uncoil in a natural roll-out type of action, with the fingers pointing toward the ball if you wish. This overall motion provides greater shoulder rotation and more rhythm. Remember, in some ways it's even more critical to unwind your body on an overhead than on a serve, since the ball is always dropping fast on an overhead and you have to make sure that you hit up on it.

Notice the role of the left hand in the adjoining photographs. I cradle the racket with this hand on the backswing [8-6], which automatically helps me coil the upper body, and then the hand comes against my body to help stop the front shoulder just before impact [8-8], which allows the racket head to accelerate—just as on the serve.

[8-8]

CHAPTER 9

The Lob

THE PROBLEM

"I never seem to fool my opponent with a lob."

A well-disguised lob, posing as a baseline drive until the last instant, can "freeze" your opponent at the net and delay his first step toward the ball. Conversely, by signaling your intentions to lob, you give an observant opponent extra time to retreat and then bomb your weaker efforts. It also frees him to volley more aggressively up at the net, knowing that he won't get caught flat-footed by an unexpected lob. So when you practice, make sure you work on your deception.

REASON:

You are telegraphing your lob by sitting back on your back foot and dropping the racket head low, with the strings laid back, well before you contact the ball [9-1].

CURE:

Try to disguise your intended lob as a passing shot until the last moment. Rotate your front shoulder away from the net, step into the ball, and swing with a low-to-high motion, as though you are about to hit a regular baseline drive, either a forehand or a backhand [9-2 through 9-4]. Always try to visualize how you look to your opponent as you learn to conceal your drive/lob intentions. If you can make a volleyer believe you're about to drive the ball, he'll come closer to the net and be more vulnerable to your lob.

[9-1]

[9-3]
[9-2] [9-4]

131

THE PROBLEM

"My lobs keep landing beyond the baseline."

REASONS:

A. You may be swinging too hard in relation to the angle of your low-to-high swing into the ball and to the amount your racket face is beveled (laid back) at impact.

B. The ball may not be traveling high enough in relation to how hard you are swinging. Most people fail to lob with enough height—ideally 30 to 40 feet over the net on a defensive lob.

CURES:

A and B. Since you should always try to swing with the same speed as you lob (unless you're scrambling just to stay alive in the rally), adjust the upward angle of your swing—not the racket bevel—to bring the ball in shorter. For example, if your previous lob was ten feet long, try swinging with the same racket-head speed, but hit with a steeper forward-and-upward stroking motion so you hit a higher lob. That ten feet in length is now ten feet in height, and the ball should land inside the baseline.

Also keep in mind that if you're going to make an error, you should strive to be too long with your lob rather than too short. You may get a lucky line call, and you won't give your opponent an opportunity for a put-away overhead. One other tip: if you're near one of your baseline corners, try to lob on the diagonal to gain extra distance and thus more time to move into good position for your next shot.

THE PROBLEM

"I lob great in practice, but I'm erratic when I play."

REASON:

If you're conscientious about practicing the lob, but the shot often fails you during a match, I'll bet you're practicing in an unrealistic way — hitting lobs from a stationary position at the center of the court behind the baseline.

CURES:

As much as possible, try to practice your lobs as you'll be expected to perform them under match-play conditions. For example:

▶ Have your practice partner hit balls that force you to lob on the move as you run along the baseline and off the court.

▶ When you're driven wide off the court, pretend that your opponent has stayed back and that you want to "buy time" to recover by hitting a deep cross-court lob.

▶ Strive to hit target areas four to six feet inside the baseline, but don't let them be your primary focus as you hit. Instead, visualize your target windows high over the net (indicated by the rebound net in 9-5) and learn how high you must hit the ball by observing where the ball lands relative to the speed and upward angle of your swing. Some of my students find it helpful to imagine hitting through a window frame at the top of their follow-through.

▶ Work on following your lob to the net, as you should do during a match whenever you force your opponent to retreat from the net to the baseline. Follow him step for step so you gain the net and put all the pressure on him to hit a perfect return shot.

▶ Practice your deception. When you run for the ball, visualize what you look like to your opponent as you try to camouflage your lob by stepping forward and taking a regular groundstroke backswing.

▶ Vary your shots from the baseline, mixing in lobs and drives so you can test your lob's progress.

[9-5]

THE PROBLEM

"My lobs are weak and ineffective."

REASON:

Very likely you are jabbing or poking at the ball instead of taking a full swing. "Jabbers" tend to slow their rackets down just before impact, afraid to come through forcefully [9-6].

CURE:

Hit forward through the ball with a low-to-high motion [9-7] and complete your follow-through, just as you should be doing on regular groundstrokes. This will keep you from slowing your swing and jabbing at the ball. A high follow-through doesn't actually guide the ball where you want it to go, since the ball leaves the strings at the instant of impact. But this effort to finish high promotes and completes a desired stroking motion that helps you lob with depth, accuracy, and confidence. So go to work on your technique and learn how an effective lob can dramatically improve your game.

[9-6]

[9-7]

THE PROBLEM

"Most of my lobs are too short, especially when I'm under pressure."

A well-timed lob can be a devastating weapon, but not when you hit the ball shallow and hand your opponent an easy overhead kill that forces you to run for cover.

REASONS:

A. If your lob is both low and short, you're swinging on too flat a plane into the ball, with insufficient racket speed. A short but high lob generally stems from having the racket face beveled back too much at impact.

B. You may simply not be hitting the ball hard enough, for any one of a number of reasons:

▶ You may be looking at your opponent out of the corner of your eye, a distraction that can cause you to unconsciously slow up your swing and pull away from the shot before impact, resulting in a more horizontal stroke.

▶ You may be getting caught in this trap: when you hit too long on your first lob of the match—perhaps ten feet past the baseline—a typical reaction is to think, "Jeez, that's terrible; I've got to ease up." So you baby your next lob, and it comes up way too short. Your opponent proceeds to deck this easy overhead, and now you're inhibited for the rest of the match.

▶ When you run laterally or retreat backward for the ball and throw up a lob, you may not be compensating for the fact that your energy flow is going away from your intended target area. This can easily cause your lobs to come up short.

CURES:

A. To help ensure a good, deep defensive lob, safely over your opponent's head and outside his overhead range, strive to swing upward at about a 55- to 60-degree angle and experiment by having the racket face beveled or tilted back anywhere up to about 45 degrees at impact.

B. To help yourself lob the ball with greater authority, whatever the pressure:

▶ Block your opponent out of your peripheral vision as you go to hit so you're free to concentrate on hitting through the ball and completing your stroke.

▶ Your proper approach to the lob should start during warm-ups before a match. Consciously hit your lobs long, then work your way in, adjusting by swinging at a steeper upward angle but at the same speed. Once the match begins, try to hit your first lob *beyond* the baseline. That may sound odd, but you'll find that lobs rarely travel as far as you think they will, and your ball will very likely stay in bounds. If it does go long, it means that you have the desired racket speed, so just elevate your next lob at a steeper angle.

▶ Similarly, try to lob five feet past the baseline when you are running off court, and notice how often the ball actually lands in play.

Further information about Vic Braden's Tennis College and Vic's earlier books, videotapes, and audio cassettes can be obtained by writing to:

The Vic Braden Tennis College
1 Coto de Caza Drive
Coto de Caza, CA 92679
Telephone: (714) 581-2990